WHAT ARE THEY SAYING ABOUT
BIBLICAL INSPIRATION?

What Are They Saying About
Biblical Inspiration?

MARK J. ZIA

Paulist Press
New York/Mahwah, NJ

Cover design by James Brisson

Library of Congress Cataloging-in-Publication Data

Zia, Mark J.
    What are they saying about biblical inspiration? / Mark J. Zia.
        p. cm.
    Includes bibliographical references.
    ISBN 978-0-8091-4699-4 (alk. paper)
    1. Bible—Inspiration. I. Title.
    BS480.Z53 2011
    220.1′3—dc22

                                                            2010042910

Published by Paulist Press
997 Macarthur Boulevard
Mahwah, New Jersey 07430

www.paulistpress.com

Printed and bound in the
United States of America

CONTENTS

INTRODUCTION

Overview

The theme of this study is the doctrine of biblical inspiration as developed and understood within Anglo-American scholarship over the past forty years. The goals of this study are threefold:

1. To present the concept of biblical inspiration as understood by significant Anglo-American scholars of various religious traditions, and hence to shed light on the *status quaestionis*.
2. To offer a gentle critique of the theories developed or maintained by these scholars.
3. To offer some modest considerations toward a fuller and more dynamic understanding of the doctrine of biblical inspiration.

Almost fifty years ago, Karl Rahner wrote, "...on the average, Roman Catholic Scripture scholars, although by no means denying or doubting the inspiration of the Bible, prefer not to touch it at all in their exegetical work,"[1] and James Barr notes:

There is no subject that has undergone greater convulsions in the last twenty-five years or that has suffered

1

greater changes in its status and esteem than biblical theology. The years immediately following the Second World War saw it rising into pre-eminence and taking over much of the leadership in biblical studies....Its high point was in the decade from 1950 to 1960.[2]

Given the typically disinterested relationship that existed between the insights of theologians and the efforts of exegetes, very few insights of Catholic scholars on the theme of biblical inspiration have found concrete expression. This observation is evidenced by the fact that only two Catholic theologians are included in this study, both of them priests. Father James Burtchaell and the late Father Bruce Vawter are the only representatives from the Catholic tradition who have made a substantial contribution to Anglo-American scholarship on the theme of biblical inspiration since the time of the Second Vatican Council. This observation is even more striking when we consider Barr's further observation that the only representative groups that even seriously consider addressing the issue of biblical inspiration are Roman Catholic and Protestant fundamentalist scholars.[3]

Yet such deficiencies are by no means limited to Catholic scholars. Childs writes, "The Biblical Theology Movement underwent a period of slow dissolution beginning in the late fifties. The breakdown resulted from pressure from inside and outside the movement that brought it to a virtual end as a major force in American theology in the early sixties,"[4] and Paul J. Achtemeier aptly points out, "...it is surprising and puzzling that discussion of the doctrine of inspiration has often been notable more by its absence than by its presence. It has been honored by being ignored in many circles."[5] Given the centrality within all Christian churches of the theme of biblical inspiration for a proper understanding of the Bible, the accessible literature on the topic suggests that the issue of inspiration is of a greater fundamental importance to Protestant Christianity than to Catholicism. The reason for the greater motivation among Protestant scholars to consider the theme of biblical inspiration seems to be linked to the unparalleled authority given to the Bible in Protestantism in the absence of an equally authoritative tradition. James Barr shares this insight in stating,

> ...the concept of inspiration has been much used in Roman Catholicism as well as in conservative Protestantism; but it has been more creatively and flexibly handled in Roman theology, doubtless because in it scripture is only one of the basic theological norms (tradition being the other) and not the sole such norm (as in conservative Protestantism).[6]

Moreover, faithful Catholics trust in the doctrinal decisions of the magisterium as true interpretations of the content of God's revelation to mankind, yet when such an authority is removed and the *sola scriptura*[7] principle substituted in its place, there is a real danger of misconstruing the revelation found in the Bible through private interpretation, which runs the risk of being erroneous. Thus a clearer understanding of biblical inspiration will enable Christians—Protestant as well as Catholic and Orthodox—to be better equipped to interpret the Scriptures according to the mind of Christ.

Choice of Authors

Six Anglo-American authors and scholars have been selected for the purpose of presenting and analyzing their contributions to the question of biblical inspiration. As with any study of this kind, the selection of some authors at the expense of others is inescapable, yet the choice of authors to be included in this study was not arbitrary. Collectively, these scholars represent and articulate in one way or another the most significant variations on our theme, thereby providing a veritable cross-section of insight to illuminate the *status quaestionis* as developed within several different Christian professions. Each of the scholars included in our study did not simply write occasional articles on biblical inspiration or contribute a chapter in a scholarly publication devoted to biblical inspiration; rather each made a specific contribution by way of a published and well-received work on the theme of biblical inspiration.

Additionally, the authors who were chosen flourished in the period from the Second Vatican Council onward. This time span was chosen for two main reasons: First, the work of Burtchaell encompasses the major trends in Catholic scholarship pertinent to biblical inspiration as articulated over a two-hundred-year period, culminating in the 1960s. This present work can be viewed as a modest continuation of Burtchaell's study, although this work focuses largely on contributions by non-Catholic scholars, whereas Burtchaell's work focused upon Catholic scholars exclusively. Second, the Constitution on Divine Revelation of the Second Vatican Council would undoubtedly have had an effect on the thoughts of the scholars included in this study. Although non-Catholic scholars would not look to this Constitution as authoritative for their work, it would, nonetheless, be necessary for them to understand what the Council was teaching and how scholarship on the theme of biblical inspiration would be affected by it.

Abraham Heschel, a Jewish rabbi, was selected for his insights into prophetic inspiration, resulting in his unrivaled opus, *The Prophets*. James Burtchaell and Bruce Vawter, Catholic priests, were chosen because they appear in virtually every bibliography for studying the theme of biblical inspiration. The Methodist elder and scholar, William J. Abraham, was selected because his work on biblical inspiration is also recognized as a sine qua non for grasping the central aspects of the doctrine of biblical inspiration.

Kern Robert Trembath, an Episcopal scholar, was chosen for his work that draws together the main currents of scholarship pertaining to biblical inspiration from within the transdenominational sphere of American Evangelicalism. Above all, his work sets forth the view of biblical inspiration as understood existentially, a hallmark of Evangelical theology of inspiration. The Presbyterian scholar P. J. Achtemeier, who also appears in many bibliographies for the doctrine of biblical inspiration, was selected for his assessment of tradition as an essential component of biblical inspiration, thus adding to the range of considerations offered by Anglo-American scholars.

The scholars will be studied in chronological order according to the publication date of their most significant contributions to our theme, beginning with the late Rabbi Abraham Heschel's work on prophetic inspiration.

1

ABRAHAM JOSHUA HESCHEL
ON PROPHETIC INSPIRATION

Introduction

Abraham Heschel, the son in a tradition of Hasidic rabbis, was born in Warsaw, Poland, on January 11, 1907, and died on the Sabbath of December 23, 1972. His masterful work on the prophets, *Die Prophetie*, was his doctoral dissertation for which he earned a PhD from the University of Berlin. After being deported from Germany by the Nazis, he went back to Poland and was appointed associate professor of philosophy and rabbinic studies at the Hebrew Union College in Cincinnati, Ohio. He went on to become a professor of Jewish ethics and mysticism at the Jewish Theological Seminary of America in New York from 1945 until his death in 1972, and was the first Jewish person to teach at Union Theological Seminary in New York during his appointment of 1965–66. A friend of Martin Luther King, Heschel was a strong advocate for ending racial discrimination and was strongly opposed on religious grounds to the Vietnam war.

Heschel sought to restore a proper understanding of God's act and man's response within the context of the biblical prophets.[1] He shows that the dynamics at work between the prophets and God consist of revelation and response, event and experience, divine initiative and free human activity. Heschel's goal is:

...to attain an understanding of the prophet through
an analysis and description of his consciousness, to
relate what came to pass in his life—facing man, being
faced by God—as reflected and affirmed in his
mind....By consciousness...I mean here not only the
perception of particular moments of inspiration, but
also of the totality of impressions, thoughts, and feel-
ings which make up the prophet's being.[2]

Unlike the other authors included in this study, Heschel
does not comment upon the various theories of inspiration.
Instead, he sets aside the question of "how" inspiration is accomplished in order to answer the question of "what does it mean for
God to inspire?" He writes:

The essence of our faith in the sanctity of the Bible is
that its words contain that which God wants us to
know and to fulfill. How these words were written
down is not the fundamental problem. This is why the
theme of Biblical criticism is not the theme of faith,
just as the question of whether the lightning and thun-
der at Sinai were a natural phenomenon or not is irrelevant to our faith in revelation.[3]

Whereas some scholars maintain that we can have no insight
into the psychological dimensions of prophetic inspiration,[4] Heschel
succeeds in probing and unfolding the consciousness of the
prophet in order to uncover some aspects of the psychological
dimension of biblical inspiration. Ultimately, Heschel identifies
the communication of the divine pathos as the overarching purpose for inspiration and seeks to probe the relationship between
the divine pathos and the consciousness of the prophet who
encounters it.

The Mission of the Prophet

Heschel writes, "...the main task of prophetic thinking is to bring the world into divine focus"[5] and notes that "Prophecy consists in the inspired communication of divine attitudes to the prophetic consciousness."[6] Contrary to the more commonly accepted view that the prophet is God's "mouthpiece" who communicates the content that God reveals to him apart from any personal interest or involvement, Heschel boldly argues, "The prophet is not a mouthpiece, but a person; not an instrument, but a partner, an associate of God. Emotional detachment would be understandable only if there were a command which required the suppression of emotion, forbidding one to serve God 'with all your heart, with all your soul, with all your might.'"[7]

The prophet does not and cannot remain a mere spectator, an indifferent messenger, but truly becomes immersed in his prophetic mission. Heschel affirms that "The prophet claims to be far more than a messenger. He is a person who stands in the presence of God (Jer 15:19), who stands 'in the council of the Lord' (Jer 23:18), who is a participant, as it were, in the council of God, not a bearer of dispatches whose function is limited to being sent on errands."[8] Moreover, the message of the prophet is for the sake of the whole people, and in receiving, understanding, and experiencing the message, the prophet truly becomes a participant in the people's drama.[9]

Heschel comments that not only is the prophet truly involved in the affairs of the people, but ultimately so also is God himself, who is at the origin of the prophetic call and mandate. For Heschel, this dynamic is at the heart of biblical inspiration and is most powerfully understood through a consideration of the divine pathos. Heschel writes, "The divine pathos is the key to inspired prophecy. God is involved in the life of man,"[10] and he further notes, "according to the biblical understanding of history, the idea of pathos is as central as the idea of man being an image of God is for the understanding of creation."[11]

Divine Pathos

Overview

   Heschel directs our attention to the fact that the prophets never spoke of God in a distant or aloof fashion, but always as being directly involved in our human state of affairs. This drama consists not so much of the revelation of the nature of God, but rather in God's concern for man; not in a revelation of dogmas and truths about God, but in a sharing in the presence of God and achieving of fellowship with him. Heschel observes that the prophets "could not use the language of *essence*; they had to use the language of *presence*. They did not try to depict Him; they tried to present Him, to make Him present. In such an effort, only words of grandeur and intensity, not abstractions, can be of any avail."[12]

   God is not the disinterested clockwork God of the Deists, but a most providential God who makes the concerns of man his own. Heschel writes:

   Most theories of religion start out with defining the religious situation as man's search for God and maintain the axiom that God is silent, hidden and unconcerned for man's search for Him. Now, in adopting that axiom, the answer is given before the question is asked. To biblical thinking, the definition is incomplete and the axiom false. The Bible speaks not only of man's search for God but also of God's search for man.[13]

   This concern and search for man by God is characteristic of divine pathos, which Heschel refers to as a central category of the prophetic understanding of God, echoed in almost every prophetic statement.[14] Heschel adds, "The divine pathos embraces all life, past, present, and future; all things and events have reference to Him. It is a concern that has the attribute of eternity, transcending all history, as well as the attribute of universality, embracing all nations, encompassing animals as well as human beings."[15]

When Heschel speaks of divine pathos, he does not speak of a passion in the sense of either a "psychological state of the soul" or in the sense of an "unreasoned emotion." Neither does he consider divine pathos to be an attribute of God, since divine pathos always expresses a relation to man. Divine pathos is "an act formed with intention, depending on free will, the result of decision and determination"[16] and is occasioned by man's deeds in human history. In other words, the divine pathos is an act of God relative to the situation of mankind. This act, freely willed by God, is not necessitated by man's condition, but rather man's condition gives the occasion for God to freely act in such a way as to manifest his deep, providential concern for the plight of man.

Heschel clarifies that the divine pathos is not to be identified with the theme of divine passion, which is found in many pagan religions, such as those of Mesopotamia, Egypt, Greece, and Rome. He writes, "In passion, the divinity is thought of as a martyr, the basis of whose suffering lies, in the last analysis, in the powerlessness of the god....Passion is the personal and private suffering of the deity; it all happens within the life of the deity, though it is taken as an event that affects the life of man."[17] On the contrary, "God is thought of as the supreme Master of heaven and earth, Who is emotionally affected by the conduct of man....Suffering is [spoken of] in the sense of compassion or in the sense of moral indignation.... Pathos is a relative state, it always refers to humanity; it is a reaction to what happens within the life of humanity."[18]

The grand premise of divine pathos is that God is willing to be involved in the world and in the history of man such that the predicament of man becomes a predicament to God himself. The almighty God is personally and intimately involved in the human drama of existence to the extent that, following biblical imagery, "man's deeds may move Him, affect Him, grieve Him or, on the other hand, gladden and please Him. This notion that God can be intimately affected, that He possesses not merely intelligence and will, but also pathos, basically defines the prophetic consciousness of God."[19]

Challenges to the Category of Divine Pathos

Heschel maintains, "In order to conceive of God not as an onlooker but as a participant, to conceive of man not as an idea in the mind of God but as a concern, the category of divine pathos is an indispensable implication. To the biblical mind the conception of God as detached and unemotional is totally alien."[20] Heschel points out that although theologians usually use concepts such as goodness and justice in forming biblical images of God, such concepts "are surpassed by statements referring to God's pathos, which, however, for a variety of reasons, has never been accorded proper recognition in the history of biblical theology."[21] Heschel writes,

> For more than two thousand years Jewish and later
> Christian theologians have been deeply embarrassed
> by the constant references in the Bible to the divine
> pathos. What were the reasons for that embarrass-
> ment? Why did they oppose the idea of pathos? The
> opposition, it seems, was due to a combination of
> philosophical presuppositions which have their origin
> in classical Greek thinking.[22]

Although the references in the Bible to the divine pathos are inescapable, the majority of theologians view such statements not as indicating a true dimension of God, but as a way in which God is accommodating man's intelligence through the application of concepts that are meaningful to man. Thus "The pedagogical interpretation of biblical anthropopathy became one of the standard solutions of the problem [of the divine pathos] in Jewish and Christian literature."[23]

At the origin of the rejection of the divine pathos, Heschel identifies Xenophanes, who insisted "that omnipotence implies repose, absolute calm, and immobility,"[24] and Parmenides of Elea, of whom Heschel writes, "...his theory of absolute being and its predicates were again and again adopted as a basis for philosophical theology. Most speculation on the nature of God held unchangeableness to be an essential attribute."[25] These currents of thought continued through Aristotle and made their entrance into Christianity largely through Aquinas's adaptation of Aristotle.

Heschel's Response

Mindful of these challenges to the category of the divine pathos, Heschel responds:

> God's unconditional concern for justice is not an anthropomorphism. Rather, man's concern for justice is a theomorphism. Human reason, a feeble reflection, reminder, and intimation of the infinite wisdom deciphered in God's creation, is not the form after which our concept of God's wisdom is modeled. The language the prophets employed to describe the supreme concern was an anthropomorphism to end all anthropomorphisms.[26]

In other words, Heschel maintains that when we speak of God as merciful, just, and kind, we are not merely using the human phenomenon in an attempt to say something meaningful about God, but rather that God is first and foremost the one who is merciful, just, and kind; therefore it is only insofar as humanity participates in these qualities that properly belong to God that we can speak of a merciful woman, a just man, and so forth. In this view, the classical way of thinking is turned upside down. Heschel explains:

> The idea of the divine pathos combining absolute self-lessness with supreme concern for the poor and the

exploited can hardly be regarded as the attribution of human characteristics. Where is the man who is endowed with such characteristics? Nowhere in the Bible is man characterized as merciful, gracious, slow to anger, abundant in love and truth, keeping love to the thousandth generation. *Pathos is a thought that bears a resemblance to an aspect of divine reality as related to the world of man. As a theological category, it is a genuine insight into God's relatedness to man, rather than a projection of human traits into divinity,* as found for example in the god of images and mythology.[27]

In response to the classical objection to the category of divine pathos, Heschel raises a powerful question: "One might wonder whether Xenophanes, had he been faced by the Bible instead of by Homer, would have felt compelled to protest against the humanization of divinity."[28] In other words, Heschel suggests that the primary objection leveled against anthropopathy by the classic Greek thinkers was not so much of a philosophical or theological nature, but of a moral one, since the only experience of anthropopathy in Greek literature is of ascribing the *negative* characteristics of man unto the gods, such as lust, envy, deception, selfishness, and other evils. Heschel observes:

Plato denounced the caprice and corruptibility of the gods, from whom the wicked could secure immunity from chastisement by means of soothing entreaties and offerings. The conception that jealousy or envy was inherent in the very nature of the gods was particularly repulsive to both Plato and Aristotle. "Thine is unwisdom, or injustice thine," says Amphitryon to Zeus. And Theseus is even more specific about the gods, "Have they not linked them in unlawful bonds of wedlock, and with chains, to win them thrones, outraged their fathers? In Olympus still they dwelt, by their transgressions unabashed."[29]

Heschel reflects, "In this sense, truly to personify the gods was to disparage them."[30] He seems to suggest that had the gods been ascribed the positive qualities of humanity instead of negative qualities, classical objections to anthropopathy may not have been so severe.

The Prophetic Act

Now that sufficient attention has been given to the category of the divine pathos and its central importance for a full understanding of prophetic inspiration, we will turn our attention to the prophetic act itself, whereby the divine pathos is encountered by the prophetic consciousness and communicated to the people. The question we seek to address is, "What is, to the mind of the prophets, the ultimate, irreducible form or essential structure of the prophetic act?"[31]

Heschel answers: "To the consciousness of the prophet, the prophetic act is more than an experience; it is an objective *event*. This is its essential form. Whatever be the motive or content, and whatever be the mode in which inspiration is apprehended, there remains always its character as an event, not as a process."[32]

In his answer, Heschel addresses two issues. First, as event, the reality of prophetic inspiration is not simply an abstract, cognitive phenomenon that deals only with propositions, but an engaging personal encounter that permeates the very being of the prophet. Heschel makes a comparison to underscore this point: "The God of the philosopher is a concept derived from abstract ideas; the God of the prophets is derived from acts and events. The root of Jewish faith is, therefore, not a comprehension of abstract principles but an inner attachment to sacred events."[33]

Second, Heschel distinguishes the unique status of prophetic inspiration as an event from the commonplace understanding of inspiration as a vague process. He goes on to explain that a process denotes regularity, yet an event is extraordinary and unique. The phenomenon of inspiration received by the prophet must not be reduced to an "everyday" occurrence or to a naturalistic understanding, but affirmed as a divine action that is "quite remote from the daily experience of modern man today."[34]

Heschel identifies two components of the prophetic act corresponding to the agents involved: namely, God and the prophet. Heschel writes, "...there are two aspects to inspiration as seen from the prophet's point of view: a moment of decision, or a turning, and a moment of expression, a direction."[35] The moment of decision, or turning, is initiated by God's will to communicate to the prophet, which Heschel calls the anthropotropic dimension of the religious event of inspiration, to which belongs:

> ...the consciousness of being approached by God, directly or indirectly, of receiving teaching or guidance, a word or an intimation; the consciousness of living under a God Who calls upon man, turns to him, is in need of him. In anthropotropic experience, man is affected by the impact of events which he does not initiate, but which are addressed to him or relate to his existence, and in which he feels a transcendent attentiveness focused upon himself.[36]

The second component of the religious event of inspiration is what Heschel calls theotropism, which refers to both the prophet's direction of God's message to the people, as well as the summons for the people to repent and convert, thereby "turning towards God" once more. We can trace the event of prophetic inspiration as follows: God inspires the prophet by communicating to him his deep concern for man, and since prophets are only sent to the wayward, this concern is due to man's departure from the covenant. Upon hearing the message of the prophet, the people are confronted with a choice: either to persist in their sins, or to accept the summons to repentance. According to this model of Heschel's, the ultimate purpose for inspiration is the salvation of God's people who have turned from him and are on the path to destruction.

It is also noteworthy that a dimension of this second component of the religious event of inspiration is that the prophet, like God, also experiences a true concern for the people; the prophet's sympathy for the people's condition is a result of his encounter with God and the revelation of the divine pathos. Heschel writes,

> It is no mere listening to, and conveying of, a divine message which distinguishes his [the prophet's] personal life. The prophet not only hears and apprehends the divine pathos; he is convulsed by it to the depths of his soul. His service of the divine word is not carried out through mental appropriation, but through the harmony of his being with its fundamental intention and emotional content.[37]

To summarize the key aspects of the prophetic act according to Heschel:[38] First, inspiration comes to the prophet as a grace, and not as either an earned reward or a sought-after reality. Second, prophetic inspiration clearly issues forth from God himself. Third, prophetic inspiration is an event, therefore it has a beginning and end point with a definite content. Fourth, the subject matter of prophecy is a real concern to God, and it is never initiated solely to convey general information. Fifth, the prophet does not simply receive a cognitive communication from God, but actively experiences the encounter with God and experiences true sympathy for the plight of man.

Concluding Reflections

Heschel has made his case for a return to a biblically grounded philosophy in an age dominated, on one hand, by an overly strict adherence to Aristotelian-Thomistic categories, and on the other hand, a deconstruction of all traditionally accepted methods of philosophical theology as expressed through postmodernism. He maintains that by focusing more on what he coined "depth theology" and focusing less on rigid dogmaticism, the modern mind will be better prepared to understand the biblical teachings concerning the nature of God who reveals and of man who is his perpetual concern.

In his study of the prophetic consciousness, Heschel has identified two components of biblical prophecy. The first component, the divine pathos, is at the core of prophetic inspiration and serves to express the great concern God has for man and the continual search of God for man to return to him. The second component, sympathy, relates to the prophet's reception, encounter, and reaction to the divine pathos as he directs the message of God to his audience.

Ultimately, the phenomenon of prophetic inspiration goes beyond the scope of a purely scientific, cultural, psychological, or social explanation, as well as transcends the limitations of the scientific method itself. All attempts to reduce the supernatural reality of biblical prophecy to the level of the natural are bound to disappoint.

A weakness of Heschel's insights lies in the fact that he addresses biblical inspiration solely from the perspective of prophetic inspiration, thereby raising the unanswered question of how such a model, in his view, can be directly applied to the nonprophetic literature of the Bible, especially to the Christian Gospels and New Testament epistles. Moreover, he does not address the question of how the inspiration of the written prophetic literature relates to the status of that same content as considered in its original oral phase prior to its inscripturation.[39]

Additionally, Heschel's exclusive stress upon the act and structure of faith is detrimental to the equal importance of the content of that faith. As we have seen, he is critical of the advances and implementation of Greek philosophy into Western metaphysics, maintaining that the intellectual structure by which the ancients understood the Bible is utterly foreign to Hellenistic thought. His implication is that we can never successfully understand the intentions and purposes beyond the Hebrew Bible unless we abandon Western notions of epistemology and return to a properly "biblical epistemology."

Especially in Catholic theology, there has always been a complementarity between faith and reason, the former built upon, perfecting, and presupposing the latter.[40] St. Anselm defined theology as "faith seeking understanding,"[41] and St. Augustine affirms, "*Intellige ut credas: crede, ut intelligas.*"[42] It is precisely in the tradition of Greek epistemology and metaphysics that, if historical experience be observed, we are better able to express and apprehend various dimensions of our faith, and to do so is fulfilling the Creator's purpose for endowing us with an intellect, so that we can actively seek and strive to understand the truth, which is ultimately grounded in God.

2
J. T. BURTCHAELL ON CATHOLIC THEORIES OF BIBLICAL INSPIRATION

Introduction

James Tunstead Burtchaell, an outspoken spokesman for the pro-life movement and a priest of the Congregation of the Holy Cross, had a career at the University of Notre Dame spanning twenty-five years. Burtchaell's main work on inspiration is entitled *Catholic Theories of Biblical Inspiration Since 1810: A Review and Critique* (Cambridge: Cambridge University Press, 1969), which is a revised version of his 1968 doctoral dissertation at Cambridge University.

J. T. Burtchaell remarks, "The controversy over biblical inspiration is an excellent test case whereby to diagnose many of the ills that have weakened Catholic theology, especially since the Reformation. The real issue here is what confounds scholars in so many areas: the manner in which individual human events are jointly caused by both God and man."[1] Burtchaell traces the history of key doctrines of biblical inspiration of the last several centuries and addresses notable, yet covert, factors responsible for the lack of progress by Catholic scholars, including "an uncritical defense of official authority...and a crude theology of divine-human collaboration."[2]

Regarding the first factor, Burtchaell singles out the combination of the magisterium and theologians who exercised their authority in limiting the range of acceptable possibilities in formulating a thorough explanation of the doctrine of biblical inspiration.[3] Burtchaell perceives the pronouncements of Rome, whether through encyclicals or through the Biblical Commission,[4] not as helpful and instructive, but as restrictive of academic inquiry and stultifying upon intellectual progress.[5]

Regarding the second factor, Burtchaell writes that many theologians had fallen prey to the misguided belief that the Bible is either all divine or all human, just as the past Christological heresies of Docetism and Arianism falsely excluded either Jesus' true humanity or his true divinity. Attempting to view the Bible on its own terms, Burtchaell traces the history of two of the most popular theories of biblical inspiration: content inspiration and verbal inspiration.

Content Inspiration

Regarding the theory of content inspiration (known also in German as *Realinspiration* and in Latin as the *res et sententiae* theory), Burtchaell observes, "Of all the theological systems which we shall have occasion to consider, none was more widely taught or more firmly assured of its respectability than the theory of content inspiration promoted by the Jesuit theologians during the latter half of the 19th century."[6] This theory, which was favored by theologians (but not by exegetes) enjoyed "a virtual monopoly in Catholic theology manuals from the 1840s until the 1890s,"[7] and maintains that the ideas found in the Bible are of divine origin, while the words are properly said to be that of man. Many theologians agreed that "having established the fact of inspiration from the declarations of tradition, and the universality of inspiration from the decrees of Trent and Vatican [I]…it would be gratuitous to insist that this inspiration need extend beyond the thoughts, or substance, of Scripture."[8] Perhaps the most forceful articulation of the content inspiration theory was by the Jesuit Giovanne Perrone of the Roman College, who perceived this new theory as a powerful alternative to the classical theory of the divine dictation of the Scriptures.

Perrone calls to mind several objections that have been raised against the dictation theory, including: God would not "need" to dictate to an author that which the author already knew via natural knowledge; the diversity of styles found in the Bible is not what one would expect if one author (God) dictated the whole;[9] like events are reported by the authors in differing ways; some of the biblical authors state that they have put considerable effort into their writing, which would not be true if they simply wrote down what another dictated to them.[10] Perrone argued for a theory of inspiration that allowed man to be more active in the process and concluded that this process would involve the activity of God implanting ideas within the author, which would then blossom and be written in a truly human way.

Other objections to the theory of divine dictation came from Francesco Patrizi, also of the Roman College, who argued that even if the divine inspiration of the Bible extended to the individual words via mechanical dictation, no translation of the Bible could claim inspiration, since the terms employed in a translation are necessarily different from those originally used. A translation properly communicates the same content as the original, but if inspiration extends beyond the content to the words themselves, as the dictation theory claims, then the substance, but not the inspiration, of the original is preserved. Considering the apparent general acceptance among the Fathers of the Church of a dictated Bible, Patrizi opines that the sense of "dictated by the Lord" so often employed by the early Christian writers was one of a "homiletic exaggeration," and although it could be argued that some portions of the Bible may have been virtually dictated to the authors, this was not the case for the majority of it.

Towering above all the others, "Far and away the most distinguished partisan of content inspiration, the theologian who most elaborately defended the theory and by whose name it is generally known, was Johann Baptist Franzelin, SJ."[11] Franzelin distinguished between the core messages of the Bible that God deemed as necessary elements of each book from the manner in which those messages were conveyed to humanity. Franzelin called the intentional elements willed by God the formal components, and the particular ways in which the core components were communicated in writing he termed the material components.

According to this model, which seeks to base itself upon the ecclesial pronouncement of Trent, *"Deus est auctor sacrorum librorum,"* the ideas found in the biblical text may be said to have been given by God, but the expression of those ideas in human language was supplied only by the human authors. Such a model was hoped to positively address the need for an established "both-and" model of biblical inspiration in relation to God's initiative and humanity's collaboration. Franzelin devised a theory that could explain the dual actions of both God and man by maximalizing God's authorship and minimalizing the human authors' contribution in a way that still preserved the true authorship of both. According to such a model, however, the acts of both God and man, although sufficient to preserve the true authorship of both, do not overlap and remain either in the divine or in the human sphere, but not in both at the same time.

As far back as beginning of the nineteenth century we find Johann Sebastian von Drey of the Tübingen School rejecting the mechanical (dictation) theory of inspiration on the grounds that "He would not accept that words or even ideas could be planted in the human mind without being actively produced in that mind."[12] Although the theory of content inspiration does rightly ascribe to the human author the necessary conditions for true authorship by leaving the choice of wording up to human ingenuity, it seems that Drey's objection still stands; while the theory of content inspiration vindicated the human author's activity in determining the words of Scripture, the content/substance of Scripture is still implanted in the mind by God without being internally produced by man. "By 1905," writes Burtchaell, "few people were dealing any more with the *res et sententiae* theory"[13] due to the advent of the new Dominican theory of verbal inspiration.

Verbal Inspiration

Franzelin and others who espoused the theory of content inspiration did not think that it was necessary to have God responsible for the actual words of the Bible, yet those who subscribed to a theory of verbal inspiration took seriously the designation of the Bible being "the *Word* of God." This new theory of verbal inspiration took its point of departure from the dictation theory by rejecting the premise that God literally dictated the words of the Bible into the ears of the human authors in a mechanical fashion, therefore the objections already leveled against the theory of mechanical dictation do not necessarily apply to this new theory of verbal inspiration since it excludes dictation. The theory of verbal inspiration is to be understood "not in the sense that God supplies and man receives a fully-elaborated statement, but that every word, just as every idea, is produced *simultaneously* and totally by the human author and the divine author."[14]

Burtchaell notes that perhaps the strongest influence in reawakening the theory of mechanical dictation from its comatose state and for modifying it into a new theory of verbal inspiration was Pope Leo XIII's mandate that the teaching and philosophical method of St. Thomas Aquinas once again take priority in Catholic seminaries.[15] Although Leo XIII never personally endorsed the theory of verbal inspiration, the theory was the fruit of Dominican theologians who attempted to postulate a thoroughly Thomistic understanding of biblical inspiration in response to the prevailing Jesuit theories. Leo XIII's mandate of Thomism was indeed far-reaching, as even the Jesuits, who were instrumental in developing the theory of content inspiration that was widely accepted among Catholic scholars, had to modify their Constitutions in 1892, "to require all members to conform to the teaching of the Angelic Doctor in all critical theological issues."[16] With the beginning of the neo-Thomistic movement, Dominicans and those favorable to a Thomistic (or neo-Thomistic) approach to biblical inspiration were now given an opportunity to bring a viable theory of biblical inspiration to the table.

The Dominican school identified a misunderstanding of the distinction between inspiration and revelation as the root problem of the theory of content inspiration. Burtchaell notes the telling statement of the exegete Eugène Lévesque: "...the fallacy [that exists within the Jesuit model of content inspiration] lies in a confusion between revelation and inspiration. The *res et sententiae* view imagines God endowing a writer with a series of ideas. But inspiration is a charism to transmit truth, not to learn it."[17]

Aquinas refers to the prophets as examples of authors who are given both inspiration and revelation, while other biblical authors were simply given the gift of inspiration alone:

> If, however, the intellectual light be divinely infused in a person, not that he may know some supernatural things, but that he may be able to judge, with the certitude of divine truth, of things that can be known by human reason, such intellectual prophecy is beneath that which is conveyed by an imaginary vision leading to a supernatural truth. It was this kind of prophecy that all those had who are included in the ranks of the prophets, who moreover were called prophets for the special reason that they exercised the prophetic calling officially. Hence they spoke as God's representatives, saying to the people: "Thus saith the Lord"; but not so the authors of the "sacred writings," several of whom treated more frequently of things that can be known by human reason, not in God's name, but in their own, yet with the assistance of the Divine light withal.[18]

According to the Jesuits, the human authors were instructed by way of ideas, and then were allowed by God to pen those ideas according to the human mode of expression proper to each author. Thus, revelation always accompanied inspiration. The Dominican view, however, did not perceive a necessity of revelation being given to the human author, since many elements in the Bible are knowable through natural reason alone. For the Dominicans, then, the emphasis regarding biblical inspiration was not upon the human author's own instruction, but on the human author's ability to transmit that instruction to future generations in a written form.

> The Thomists envision inspiration as a divine influence affecting both the will and the intellect....unlike revelation, it need not be consciously recognized by its beneficiary. More important, inspiration endows one with the gift of sure and certain judgment, while revelation infuses, in addition to this, the materials and information upon which this judgment is brought to bear.[19]

Thomists generally agree that in those cases where new knowledge was needed, revelation would accompany the inspiration of the writers. Yet in instances when human knowledge was sufficient to know the truths that God wanted, inspiration would have been operative without accompanying revelation.

Another problem with the theory of content inspiration is summarized by Edmund Ford: "The thoughts of a writer cannot advance without words and the framing of sentences, and these form a writer's style. If a human mind is under the influence of a divine inspiration while it is thinking, it is impossible for the words and style of the writer to remain outside the influence of such divine action."[20] Applying Aquinas's notion of instrumental causality, the theory of verbal inspiration affirmed that the activities of both God and man are coterminal rather than isolated:

"The Holy Spirit directs both ideas and words in the process of writing. It is precisely because he is an infinite cause that he can employ secondary causes without restricting their own freedom of action; no created cause could succeed in this. Thus, though God is responsible for the entire book, so are the human authors."[21]

As Franzelin was the exemplar of the Jesuit theory of biblical inspiration, the Dominican exegete Marie-Joseph Lagrange was the exemplar of the Dominican theory of verbal inspiration. Burtchaell draws attention to the fact that Lagrange "Thoroughly agrees that content inspiration makes its chief mistake, not in removing the wording of the Bible from God's control, but in removing the thoughts and ideas from that of man."[22] Lagrange rightly identified the inner unity between ideas and those words that are vehicles in expressing those ideas, and rejected any attempts to falsely split the two as a contrived way to satisfy the divine and human characteristics of the Bible.[23]

Aquinas's teaching on instrumental causality became the accepted framework through which Thomists like Lagrange could explain that the human authors were truly responsible for both the content and expression of the truths found in the Bible, yet the very choice of words was itself inspired by God as well. This conception differs from the older dictation method in that instead of God "speaking the words," as it were, to the authors, the authors were free to employ their own terminology and expressions, and at the same time were assured that their communication in written form was exactly as God intended.[24]

Lagrange and his fellow Dominicans made headway in advancing a more tenable theory of biblical inspiration than the previous Jesuit model of content inspiration, and by the beginning of the twentieth century, the Jesuit theory had largely lost its appeal. Burtchaell notes of this time that with the death of Pope Leo XIII and in the early years of Pope Pius X,

[During] the [Modernism] heresy scare of 1907–10 it made not a great deal of difference whether one was

wildly or mildly liberal; a wee bit of the germ was quite
enough to merit quarantine. And so, without being
condemned, without being disproven, without really
being abandoned in favor of any alternative, the theory
of verbal inspiration, which had been a-building since
about 1880, simply dropped from view.[25]

Catholic Scholarship and the Magisterium

Burtchaell refers to the promulgation of the encyclical letter
Divino afflante Spiritu by Pope Pius XII in 1943 as the "Roman
thaw" that revived the state of Catholic biblical studies after nearly
forty years of little productivity. He notes that Pierre Benoit was
one of the first scholars to take advantage of the liberties offered
by Pius XII by developing a neo-Thomistic theory of biblical
inspiration.

Addressing the problem of excessive magisterial involvement in biblical research pertaining to the question of inspiration,
Burtchaell is firmly opposed to relying on past teachings, whether
of the magisterium or even the canonical Old Testament, because
he views truth as continually evolving beyond the limitations of
past expression and situations. He acknowledges the long tradition of doctrinal integrity within the Church, but he questions
whether the tradition is correct, since it presents a static view of
truth and never advances beyond the initial and therefore primitive expression of truth. "No ancient statement or document ever
quite puts forth the truth adequately for contemporary needs. No
past statement can serve for the present in its past form; and all
present statements in their turn will forthwith become obsolete
for generations to come. We consult the past but we do not use it
for teaching...."[26] Burtchaell proposes a view regarding the nature
of the Bible that reduces it, at best, to a history lesson, and at worst,
to a fossil record of a past age:

What does the Church find in her Scriptures? As in other literature of her past, she finds what former believers had to say about God and their life in his sight. And as in that other literature, she does not expect to find a statement for the present, a perfect expression of the mind of God. Accordingly as it is a faithful reproduction of past belief, the Bible will display the imperfections, confusions, shortsightedness, inconsistency, and errors that beset believers of that era, as they are always going to afflict the faith of feeble men.[27]

Concluding Reflections

Burtchaell's solution to the problem of authority is to critically examine the Bible on its own merits through an inductive method, apart from any externally based judgments or teachings about it. He writes, "Advance would begin more surely and rapidly from the Book itself. We have little to expect from the discussions of speculative and practical judgment, the lexicographical meaning of *auctor* of the fourth century, or what literary forms are acceptable for divine use, unless we first scrutinize the Bible to see what it shows of its own nature and origins."[28]

With respect to the apparent human-divine tension in the formulation of the Scriptures, Burtchaell observes, "God is cause of human activity without himself reaching in to take control away from us."[29] Such an observation dismisses the possibility of tension between the divine and human element of the composition of Scriptures, and claims to follow after an analogy of the incarnation.[30] Burtchaell views error in the Scriptures as necessary consequences of its human dimension, and he considers it impossible that these errors could be so severe as to lead the believer away from salvation according to the divine dimension of Scripture. He writes, "In the end, we should be more accurate to say that what God has promised his Church is not certitude, but survival."[31]

The shortcomings of Burtchell's study are rooted in his conviction that the magisterium is antagonistic toward authentic biblical scholarship, and therefore he posits that there is a necessary tension between the teaching authority of the Church and the contributions of theological scholars. He presents a view that portrays the actions of the magisterium as oppressive and restrictive of scholarship, rather than encouraging of scholarship that respects the complementarity between faith and reason and acknowledges the limitations of historical-critical methods of exegesis.[32] Some relatively recent teachings concerning the diverse roles in which *all* the members of the Church, not just the clergy, may exercise the task of the interpretation of Scripture is stated in the Pontifical Biblical Commission's *Interpretation of the Bible in the Church.*[33]

As can be seen, the magisterium lauds all efforts to properly involve the entire Church in the interpretation of the Bible, mindful of the relationship that exists among the magisterium, the ordained clergy, and the laity.

3
BRUCE VAWTER ON
SOCIAL INSPIRATION

Introduction

Born in Forth Worth, Texas, in 1921, Bruce Vawter was ordained a Catholic priest in 1947 and received a doctorate in biblical studies from the Pontifical Biblical Institute in 1956. His professional career included teaching posts at De Paul University, Catholic University of America, the University of San Francisco, St. Thomas Seminary, Kenrick Seminary, and Vanderbilt University. He served as president of the Catholic Biblical Association in 1961–62 and was editor-in-chief of the *Catholic Biblical Quarterly* from 1966 through 1968.

Utilizing popular advances made through a critical study of the literary and historical dimensions of the Scriptures, Vawter's work is a historical and theological assessment of key theories of biblical inspiration from early Christianity through the twentieth century. He argues that no single model of inspiration proposed thus far does justice to the diverse genres found within the Bible, nor do most theories of inspiration frame this theory in relation to the contemporary encounter of the believer with salvation. Vawter concludes that a phenomenon as rich and complex as biblical inspiration cannot be reduced to simply one static model, regardless of how promising it may appear. He places his allegiance in the dynamic theory of social inspiration, opining that only such a theory does justice to the Bible itself and appeals to the contemporary believer.[1]

Canonical Considerations

The biblical canon is defined by Vawter as "certain works and words, committed to writing and possessing all the normal characteristics of the literary usages of their times and of their distinct authors, [which] hold a dimension for the believer that is not held by any other literature however venerated by him or even thought by him to be in this or that way superior."[2] Observing the nature of this canon, Vawter identifies its disparity as a key factor that sets it apart from the canon of any other religious literature. Rather than having the properties akin to a seamless garment, Vawter points out that the biblical canon "testifies to the diversity—theological, cultural, personal—of the minds that brought it into being"[3] and that "the disparity is not merely one of techniques and tastes, of viewpoints and options; it is also one of basic affirmations and decisions, of theologies, even of fundamental religious attitudes."[4] Vawter notes that "the fact of disparity within unity represented by the Bible and its canon was recognized by the Biblical authors themselves, and the consciousness of this fact contained the germ of the later theology of inspiration."[5]

Vawter provides several examples of how the content and form of many of the canonical biblical texts have undergone revisions over time rather than being the work of a single, unified author at a given historical period. For example, he notes how the definitive form of the Psalms, the prophetic corpus, and the Deuteronomic history resulted from the contributions of many individual and collective rereadings and editorial revisions. He observes, "...not only editors and redactors but also commentators and compilers, polemicists and counter-polemicists, rectifiers and counter-rectifiers, are among the offices we must acknowledge to have been filled by the Biblical writers who worked within the framework of what finally emerged as the canon."[6]

The Prophetic Model of Inspiration

Nearly every scholar who has written on biblical inspiration, including Vawter, identifies 2 Timothy 3:16 as the primary internal biblical basis for this doctrine. Vawter acknowledges that the direct sense of the passage pertains to the Old Testament texts, which were those books that instructed Timothy from his youth, yet he rightly agrees that Paul did not intend to exclude from inspiration the books of the New Testament that were being written. Of the term *theopneustos*, Vawter observes that it "is not 'Biblical' Greek: it comes not from the LXX but from the philosophico-religious vocabulary of classical Greek and Hellenism, where it is applied to the ecstatic mantis possessed by an alien, in the hypothesis a divine, spirit."[7]

Vawter notes that ecstatic prophecy is "a phenomenon that has occurred at one time or another in most religious movements ancient and modern, primitive or sophisticated,"[8] yet he points out that "although 2 Tim 3:16 has made use of a word borrowed from mantic experience, there is no reason at all to suppose that its author thought of the Biblical word as a product of ecstatic seizure. An assimilation of language is not, however, an assimilation of ideas."[9] Vawter explains that the classical term for "God-breathed," which found its way into the otherwise Koine New Testament, was employed due to a "linguistic syncretism"; there was simply no other term to use in its place. Of import is not the Hellenistic origin of the term, but the Hebraic idea that is represented through it.

Thus the conception invoked by *theopneustos* still retains its status as a biblical concept, even though the term itself and its classical definition are foreign to the Hebraic culture. As a biblical concept, Vawter observes that "breath, the obvious sign of the presence of life, easily came to be identified with life itself, or per-

haps more accurately with the sine qua non of the body's life."[10]
The Scriptures were never understood by the ancients to be static
and lifeless, but living, dynamic, and therefore formative for the
believing communities. In his work Vawter emphasizes this formative and therefore authoritative dimension of inspiration for the
community over and above a content or textually centered
approach that would have its terminus elsewhere than in the
inspired community.

The inspired ones par excellence of the Bible were the
prophets, who clearly identify God as the origin of their utterances. In both Judaism and early Christianity many theologians
wrote as if such prophecy were the result of verbal dictation.
Vawter argues that although many early writers appeared to subscribe to a verbal dictation theory based on how they expressed
themselves, most of them, in fact, did not believe in mechanical
dictation, a theory that is often confused with verbal dictation.
Vawter writes,

> Though in practice the Biblical word was very nearly
> always treated by the Fathers as a compendium of
> oracular utterances, in theory at least the patristic ten-
> dency was against the Greek mantis tradition as the
> explanation of spiritual prophecy. The Bible, they
> believed (even if they did not always act on the belief),
> had not been mechanically dictated to passive scribes
> but was a work produced by the Spirit of God through
> the action of charismatic men.[11]

Vawter comments that the "theory of verbal inspiration"
means "not the crude anthropomorphism of a verbal dictation but
rather the conclusion that any creative writing, inspired writing
included, must essentially be a work of word-making."[12] In this
sense, the dictation theory, which holds that the very choice of
words used in the Bible was dictated by God, cannot properly be

called a form of verbal inspiration, since no judgments resulting in "word making" would occur.

For the prophet, the meaning of biblical inspiration was understood as "the mouth of a man conscious of possessing God's word and of a moral compulsion to speak it, but of a man also actively engaged in dialogue with God, whose own spirit, and not only God's, has found expression in the record of inspiration."[13]

Vawter concludes, "it is extremely unlikely that the Hellenistic ideas of prophecy and inspiration are accepted by the NT,"[14] and when faced with the apparent problem of prophets announcing "the Word" of God, Vawter points out the sense in which "word" was understood against the Hebraic biblical background:

> Whereas in most of our modern languages and to most modern men "word" means the oral or literary means whereby some reality finds expression, this is not the case in the Semitic framework of the Bible, a framework that has been faithfully preserved in the Greek of the NT. Here "word" is rather the reality itself, always the reality primarily, regardless or even in spite of the inadequacy of its expression by mouth or pen.[15]

Vawter applies the insight he has generated regarding prophetic inspiration to the larger category of biblical inspiration. He opines, "There is no reason to suppose that the Biblical authors would have conceived their own relation to the spirit as any different from that of the Prophets to the spirit...there is much reason to suppose that they thought of these relationships in precisely the same way."[16] Yet Vawter warns of the temptation to reduce the theory of biblical inspiration to that of prophetic inspiration, as many have done. He writes, "...it is, and has long been, time that for clarity's sake we separate scriptural inspiration from the prophetic model that has confused the issue as much as it elucidated it."[17] Vawter maintains that any rigid, overly dogmatic view of inspiration attempting to explain the entire phenomenon of biblical inspiration according to one standard model does a grave injustice to the diversity of literary expressions found in the Bible.[18]

The Scholastic Synthesis and
Later Protestant Thought

Vawter describes Scholasticism as "the doctrine of the schools, the system of thinking, philosophical and theological, that dominated the intellectual life of medieval Europe."[19] He states that Scholasticism did not produce any new ideas concerning biblical inspiration, but rather reshaped, restructured, and ordered previous patristic thought under a unifying philosophical method that was not accessible to the patristic writers.[20]

Unlike the patristic era, Scholasticism

...was an age in which Christian and heathen, Jew and Muslim, Latin and Arab, anyone who chose to communicate with others at all in dialogue or controversy could do so with the presumption of sharing the same first principles and methodology and therefore—when he had been properly translated, if he was a non-Latin—of being understood at once, however much others might disagree with him.[21]

Building upon the primitive prophetic model of the patristic era, Scholasticism utilized the newly introduced philosophy of Aristotle to formulate a more accurate understanding of biblical inspiration.[22] According to the Aristotelian category of instrumental efficient causality as applied to the phenomena of biblical inspiration,

God, the principal cause, had moved the instrumental cause, the Prophet, to speak, to act or to write. The effect produced is the word of God: it is God who uttered through the Prophet, who of himself would have been incapable of it. Yet it is a word into which the Prophet also has truly entered, for it is the work of his mind and will and other faculties that the principal cause utilized and "elevated" in the process.[23]

It was not until the Second Vatican Council that the Scholastic synthesis of patristic thought resulting in the theory of instrumental efficient causality officially received its privileged status for the universal Church.[24]

The highpoint of the Scholastic period was unquestionably the systematization of earlier theological thought by St. Thomas Aquinas, who would become a sure norm of Catholic orthodoxy in philosophical and theological matters. Vawter recalls that before the time of Aquinas, especially with Augustine, divine inspiration was understood as a *habitus*, that is, a permanent, abiding character. Aquinas, however, identified divine inspiration not as a habit, but as a *motio*, that is, a temporary movement of God that would cease to be operative once the human author completed his task. When operative, this movement of God would act upon the intellect, specifically upon human judgment, supernaturally elevating it to accomplish its task of expressing God's word through human language, even if the human author might not understand the full effect of everything expressed via inspiration.

Although Vawter tends to judge Aquinas's theory, as well as the Scholastic approach to biblical inspiration in general, as too intellectual, he admits, "...however inadequate the scholastic theory of inspiration may have proved to be, it still remains for all practical purposes the only such theology that has been elaborated."[25]

The early Protestant theologians differed little from the Catholic Scholastics in the manner in which they approached their theological investigations into the Bible. However, their new objective was to demonstrate how the Bible could be said to be the supreme rule of faith, since both sacred tradition and Church authority were rejected. It would be even more crucial, then, for Protestants to demonstrate the privileged place of the Bible in the life of the Christian than for Catholics, the latter having sacred tradition and Church authority to supplement the importance of the Bible.

Martin Luther, the founder of Protestantism, personally defined the canon of inspired books to be those books that preached and conveyed Jesus Christ to the believers. Such a criterion of a "canon within the canon" allowed him to dismiss the inspiration (and therefore canonicity) of several books of the Bible, including the Deuterocanonicals and the Epistle of James. It is well known that Luther rejected James's teaching of the importance of good works in the life of the believer, initially casting aside that epistle, yet Vawter notes, "The epistle of James, which contains more allusions to the words of Jesus than any other NT work outside the gospels (G. Kittel), does emphasize an all-important aspect of NT Christology: of Jesus the magisterial ethical teacher, the Messiah (E. Käsemann)."[26] A distinctive feature of Luther's theology from that of the Scholastics, however, is the emphasis on the inner testimony of the Holy Spirit and its importance for the life of the believer. For Luther, the charism of inspiration was not simply a phenomenon that took place in the past, but one that continues in the lives of believers who encounter the Bible. This perspective sets the Bible "in relation to a dynamic and living as opposed to a static and fossilized inspired word."[27]

With the advent of lower criticism in the eighteenth and nineteenth centuries, many Protestant scholars began to cast aside preconceived notions of biblical inspiration that apparently could not be harmonized with the conclusions of textual criticism. The findings of textual criticism concluded that we could not be certain of the verbal purity of the extant manuscripts, since there exist over 200,000 variant readings in the several thousand manuscripts,[28] the earliest NT manuscript dating several centuries from the initial writing of the actual events. These findings are enough to show that if the theory of verbal inspiration is, in fact, the authentic theory concerning the operation of biblical inspiration, then the nearly countless translations of the Bible in circulation cannot claim to be inspired, nor could we claim plenary inspiration of Bibles even in the original ancient languages, since the manuscript evidence upon which they are based cannot even agree on the precise terms employed at all times.

Vawter observes that in the nineteenth century, the Bible began to be formally judged by higher criticism, which concluded that the traditional conception of individual authorship of the various books of the Bible was but a myth. In fact, literary and historical criticism concluded that far more hands and a longer textual history than previously thought were involved in composing the majority of books in the Bible. Taken to the extreme by some scholars, the Bible was gradually stripped of its inspiration, truthfulness, and ultimately its authority in the name of biblical criticism, reducing the Bible to simply one great book among others of its age.

Concluding Reflections

Vawter believes that "inspiration should be thought of primarily as one of the qualities bestowed upon the community of faith by the Spirit of God that has called it into being."[29] Given the findings of scientific criticisms, Vawter maintains that "to ask who is *the* inspired author of a text of Scripture may be to raise an invalid question,"[30] and he is convinced that one should avoid models of biblical inspiration that focus on the individual literary authors and instead focus upon a model that accounts for the larger faith community as a whole. He states, "If the reduction of all inspiration to the single prophetic model proved to be unrealizable, so too did the effort to distinguish one, two, or three kinds of inspiration, which was usually the result achieved by those who were in revolt against the inadequacies of the prophetic model."[31]

Vawter exhibits a negative attitude toward the medieval model of instrumental causality, stating, "…it seems proper to ask whether by now the traditional theology of inspiration has not rung all the possible changes on the analogy of instrumental causality. Its continued usefulness may certainly be questioned,"[32] and adds that "to analyze every last line, every particle even, of the Bible and attempt to specify the kind of divine causality that is responsible for its presence there, is an obvious impossibility."[33] The alternative model that Vawter proposes is one of social inspiration. The aspects of the social model of inspiration that address the insufficiency of the instrumental causality model and its variations are mainly two: such a model not only bypasses the problem of multiple authorship, but it also makes the biblical word relevant for the whole community of faith instead of only for the person receiving the inspiration.

Vawter accentuates the view that the Bible's ability to inspire the believing community through God's words to humanity throughout time is at the heart of the social model of inspiration. He notes, "…for some time the burning question for theology has not been an exclusive contemplation of a once-for-all writing process but an understanding of the relation of Scripture to a continuing and living word of God."[34] He identifies inspiration as an action that does not terminate in the text, nor in an individual author, but rather as a dynamic activity that embraces and bears witness to the common spiritual good of the entire believing community.[35] Vawter summarizes his theory of inspiration as follows:

> Rather than to conceive of God as acting upon an individual directly in favor of the community, we are now persuaded to think of Him as working through the community by affecting the individual. Such, in fact, is the mode of the divine activity as it is otherwise presented to us both in the Scripture and in tradition. In the OT and the NT as well the individual finds his identification as a person in confrontation with God

not as an isolated individual but as a member of the community of faith, of Israel, of the Church.[36]

Vawter affirms that an acknowledgment and proper treatment of the diverse literary genres within Scripture is indispensable for any true understanding of inspiration, noting that just as the literary genres are diverse, so too must there be more than simply one standard notion of biblical inspiration. He writes, "To attempt to perpetuate a monolithic concept of inspiration in the face of the complexity and variety of the Bible's literary history is simply to court confusion."[37] Vawter's strong opinions concerning spiritual exegesis, allegory, and elements of typology stem from his conviction that such modes of interpretation ignore or run contrary to the historical sense as communicated via the specific genres employed within the complex literary corpus of the Bible. He maintains that the social theory of inspiration does justice to the differing genres found within the Bible and is the best overall solution to the problem of biblical inspiration.

The difficulty with the theory of social inspiration is found in the fact that, according to the traditional thought of the Church, the charism of inspiration was always directed to specific, individual authors who received the fruits of this grace in a unique way, directed toward the good of the Church. Although it is true to say that the sacred authors are themselves part of the ecclesial community, and that the Holy Spirit works in the midst of the community, the operation of the Holy Spirit upon the community as a whole is quite distinct from the specific, direct, personal intervention of the Holy Spirit upon the inspired sacred authors. In the numerous documents of the Church that address the phenomenon of inspiration, direct reference is made to those individuals whose minds were enlightened, elevated, and made capable of receiving, passing judgment upon, and communicating divinely revealed truth (cf. *Dei Verbum* 12). There does not appear to be any historical or theological basis to the possibility that the charism of biblical inspiration was collectively or anonymously given. Thus whether one agrees with the position of Karl Rahner, which maintains the social inspiration of the Scriptures in the historical proximity of the early Church, or agrees with the position of J. L. McKenzie, who maintains that social inspiration is operative even following the period of the early Church through today, the weakness of the position remains the same.

4
W. J. ABRAHAM AND DIVINE INSPIRATION ACCORDING TO HUMAN ANALOGY

Introduction

A native of Belfast, Northern Ireland, William J. Abraham is currently the Albert Cook Outler Professor of Wesley Studies at the Perkins School of Theology at Southern Methodist University in Dallas, Texas, where he has taught since 1985. Abraham earned a DPhil degree at Regent's Park College of Oxford University in 1977 and a MDiv degree from Asbury Theological Seminary in 1973. Abraham, an elder of the United Methodist Church, has published several books and articles relating to his interests in religious epistemology, the doctrine of revelation and inspiration, and evangelism.[1]

Abraham acknowledges that the crisis over a proper understanding of biblical inspiration is felt even within Evangelical circles, observing, "We need to rethink and reformulate the doctrine of the inspiration of the Bible. Recent theology generally and recent Evangelical theology in particular have failed to provide an adequate account of inspiration."[2] Writing from within this Evangelical tradition, Abraham seeks to offer "a positive account of inspiration that is contemporary, coherent, and credible."[3] Abraham questions the desire of many Evangelicals to stay loyal to the "standard orthodoxy" position of inspiration as inherited from B. B. Warfield, a view that Abraham maintains is outdated and in need of reform. He argues against the legitimacy of the traditional Evangelical practice of maintaining the theory of inspiration as a central rather than secondary tenet of belief. Additionally, whereas many scholars identify inspiration with divine speaking and reduce it to that phenomenon, Abraham makes careful distinctions among the three interrelated concepts of inspiration, divine speaking, and revelation.

Divine Speaking

Much has been written, observes Abraham, pertaining to how God is said to have "spoken" through the prophets based on an inductive study of the Bible, yet there has been little or no agreement on the way in which this divine speaking is to be predicated of God with regard to its human recipients. For Abraham, such a focus on divine speaking is misplaced and ought to center upon the act of inspiration itself rather than the act of speaking in particular. Abraham writes, "If there is one mistake in recent theories of inspiration which deserves to be singled out for special attention, that mistake is at root conceptual. Rather than pause to reflect on divine inspiration, Evangelical theologians have built their theories around the idea of divine speaking. This is simply a basic category mistake."[4] Abraham does not dismiss the significance of divine speaking; he simply wants it relegated to a position of lesser importance.

Let us consider the following statement of divine speaking: "God spoke through the prophets." Abraham asks, "How are we to interpret 'speaking' when predicated of God? Are we to imagine that God spoke in an audible voice, in a fashion similar to human speaking? Or are we to think of the speech of God as something unique and interior, something that involved an inner voice, but no outer voices, say, rather like a form of telepathy?"[5] Abraham suggests that the answer to this question is more elusive than one might think, since the verb in question, "speak," cannot be used in the same sense when applied to God as when it is ascribed to human beings. He instructively observes, "As I see it, some doctrine of analogy is indispensable in any coherent account of the meaning of religious language. Without it we slide into either empty equivocation or radical agnosticism in our thinking about God."[6]

This analogy, proposes Abraham, should be applied to the event of inspiration. Abraham is aware that many theologians identify God's act of inspiration with that of speaking, but he points out that God can inspire without words, and therefore divine speaking is not an essential dimension of divine inspiration. In order to arrive at a clearer understanding of how the term "inspire" applies to God, Abraham suggests that we first examine how the term applies to human beings. Once a foundational understanding of the term as applied to humans is reached, one can then suggest, via induction, how the term may analogously be predicated of God.

Anticipating objections to his assertion that divine speaking must be included with divine action as the context by which we know God, Abraham puts forth the case of Romans 1:20–21 in which the natural knowability of God is affirmed by way of reflection upon the natural world (that is, the world considered as a manifestation of a divine act). In this case, does it not appear that we have an example of the event of creation sufficiently bearing witness to God, noting the absence of propositional importance? Abraham responds, "Creation does not provide enough to license claims as to what God is intending for mankind when he creates."[7] Again, Abraham emphasizes the importance of both act and speech in the context of divine revelation as he observes, "By telling particular people what he was doing in history, God enabled his people to grasp the revelatory significance of what took place in history. Divine action in history was thus spelled out in some details and thereby God came to be known more fully. Without this there is nothing but confusion and ambiguity."[8]

Thus Abraham dislodges the importance of divine speaking from the realm of biblical inspiration and inserts it into the sphere of revelation, arguing that it most properly belongs there. He demonstrates that without the notion of divine speaking, our understanding of divine revelation will be deficient. Indeed, "It is through God's word that we in part discover his action in history for the saving of mankind,"[9] and for Abraham, it is in light of the Bible as the record of these revelatory "speech-acts" of God that the Bible has a rightful claim to authority.

Abraham's Proposal

When we state that our God is one who acts, we are ready to follow up this proposition with concrete examples of God's activity in human history,

> …otherwise all we have is a general, if not abstract, concept that fails to relate God to the world of both everyday life and religious experience.…Without some specification of what God has done and is doing we would be left with a very general concept that would be too far removed from life and experience to be religiously satisfying.[10]

Abraham identifies some examples of God's agency in history: creation out of nothing; the liberation of the Hebrews from slavery in Egypt; the miracles of Jesus; the sending of the Holy Spirit on Pentecost; and so forth.

Carrying this idea over to the theory of inspiration, Abraham argues that the best way to establish a better-grounded concept of inspiration is to first consider the phenomenon of inspiration concretely as it is true of human persons before attempting to understand the same concept in relation to God. Abraham's methodology consists of four phases. First, he maintains that the concept of divine inspiration must be rooted in the human meaning of one person being said to inspire another. Second, he explores how, exactly, the activity of divine inspiration is carried out between human persons. Third, he analyzes elements of inspiration between humans in order to determine its necessary features. Fourth, Abraham qualifies how inspiration may be predicated of God, in light of how it has been observed to exist between human persons.

The model suggested by Abraham to accurately illustrate inspiration between humans is the student-teacher model.[11] In considering how a student (or students) may be inspired by his or her teacher, several features of inspiration are demonstrated. First, since no two students have exactly the same eagerness to learn, intellectual capacity, classroom demeanor, attention span, and the like, it follows that one student will be inspired to a greater or lesser degree than another student; inspiration is not static, but admits of degrees. Second, the student in the classroom who is being inspired does not remain passive, but attentively and actively processes and attempts to understand the content being communicated by the teacher, regardless of whether this content is communicated through words, artistic or aesthetic mediums, visual stimuli, or yet other ways. It is evident that although speech usually accompanies the act of inspiration, it is not necessary in order for inspiration to have its full effect. Third, the student is inspired in and through his or her natural intelligence, and not in a way that circumvents or replaces the student's natural faculties; inspiration does not cover or abolish the faculties of the student, but enhances them. Fourth, since classroom instruction is not an isolated phenomenon, but a dynamic environment consisting of several influences, it is not uncommon for students to make mistakes through distractions and misunderstandings as they are being inspired. It is furthermore true that students do not attribute those mistakes to the teacher, but to their own failure to completely understand or apply what has been communicated to them by the teacher.

These four primary features of the process of inspiration based on how a teacher inspires a student are helpful in formulating the concept of how God may be said to inspire. Giving further consideration to the above process, it becomes evident that inspiration occurs through other activities and is not a separate activity in itself. We would not say that a teacher is teaching one moment, then inspiring the next. Neither do we say that a teacher actively decides to inspire at one moment, then at another moment chooses to cease being inspiring so that he or she can begin to discuss the homework assignment; inspiration takes place in and through the normal activities of the teacher. This realization is of the utmost significance for Abraham and certainly is a hallmark of his unique proposal of inspiration.

After analyzing the general process of inspiration as it pertains to the student-teacher relationship, as well as the specific activity of inspiration, Abraham concludes his assessment with a consideration of two primary effects of human inspiration. First, when several people are inspired by the same agent, there will be a significant degree of unity. Yet the degree to which this unity is manifested cannot be postulated deductively. Allow me to give an example: If a professor is giving a lecture to his students covering the first three chapters of the book of Genesis, it is reasonable to assume that each student in the classroom who takes notes will write down information pertinent to those chapters of Genesis. Yet one cannot postulate deductively (that is, in advance) that every student wrote down *all* the pertinent points of the lecture that were communicated by the professor. Only after an inductive assessment of the students' notes can one determine the degree of unity present therein.

The second primary effect of human inspiration as given by Abraham is that there will not be too radical a departure from the views of the teacher among those students who have been inspired.[12] Recalling that Abraham's analogy is not simply limited to the conveyance of information between a teacher and students, but also to the dynamic event of the teacher inspiring the students, it is reasonable to assume that the students' views will closely resemble those of the teacher. Inspiration is something that one identifies as a positive and good influence, and therefore a person would naturally seek to retain what he or she has received via inspiration. In summary of the key dimensions of this analogy of inspiration, Abraham writes,

> First, inspiration is a unique, irreducible activity that takes place between personal agents, one of whom, the inspirer, makes a definite, objective difference to the work of the other, the inspired, without obliterating or rendering redundant the native activity of the other. Secondly, inspiration is a polymorphous concept in that it is achieved in, with, and through other acts that an agent performs.[13]

Based on these observations of how inspiration is effected between human persons, Abraham is able to draw conclusions as to how inspiration may be predicated of God in relation to the Bible:

> When we speak of the divine inspiration of the Bible it is legitimate to talk in terms of degrees of inspiration; to insist on the full, indeed heightened, use of native ability in the creation of style, content, vocabulary etc.; to note that there is no guarantee of inerrancy, since agents, even when inspired by God, can make mistakes; and finally to infer that inspiration will result, first, in some kind of unity within biblical literature and secondly in the committal to writing of a reliable and trustworthy account of God's revelatory and saving acts for mankind.... We must allow a genuine freedom to God as he inspires his chosen witnesses, knowing that what he does will be adequate for his saving and sanctifying purposes for our lives.[14]

Abraham establishes, on the basis of the considerations already discussed, two minimum principles that must be at the foundation of any accurate theory of biblical inspiration. Given these principles, Abraham does not deem it necessary to limit divine inspiration to the past work of developing the Bible. He maintains that divine inspiration is at work today in the life of the Christian, just as divine inspiration was involved with the coming-to-be of the biblical record.[15] His model therefore appeals to both the Biblicist and the contemporary Christian, and he believes that his model is honest in that it does not claim to know in advance of an inductive study what the Bible should or should not contain, as the deductivists maintain.[16]

In the beginning of our consideration of Abraham's position on biblical inspiration, we pointed out that Abraham rejects the identification of Evangelicalism with its extreme Fundamentalist form, and he reminds us that the term "Evangelicalism" goes back to the Protestant revivals at the time of the Reformation. Writing from within the Methodist tradition of Evangelicalism, Abraham acknowledges that he is standing on the shoulders of those who have gone before him, most notably, John Wesley.

Abraham relates three aspects of Wesley's theology that are valid for contemporary Evangelicalism and that also are in harmony with Abraham's conclusions as identified in this study. First, Wesley has no objection to an inductive approach to the Scriptures, stating that such an approach is the only one that does justice to the actual phenomenon of the Bible. Second, the theological and salvific purpose of Scripture is to communicate the mind of God to men for the sake of their salvation, thus a doctrine of biblical inspiration must be true to this purpose. Third, although the Bible is authoritative for theology, human reason and experience also play a role in the life of the believer. Abraham carries Wesley's positions over to the problem at hand of biblical inspiration and concludes, "All these concerns—to take inductive considerations seriously, to attend to the central purposes of Scripture, to draw on the wider insights of reason and experience—have been incorporated in the proposals developed earlier,"[17] yielding what he considers to be both a theologically sound and a critically honest theory of biblical inspiration.

Concluding Reflections

William J. Abraham has proposed the model of a teacher and student as a way to better understand what it means for one agent to inspire another. His motivation for proposing such a model rests in his conviction that only after understanding how the term "inspiration" is used on the natural level between human persons can we understand how it may be predicated of God. He argues that from an understanding of how one human person inspires another, we can then attempt to explain how one human person may be inspired by God.

Abraham also distinguishes divine inspiration from divine speaking, and demonstrates that God has inspired human beings in the past in a nonverbal manner. Too often, he notes, the concept of divine inspiration is reduced to verbal inspiration, which, in turn, is reduced to prophetic inspiration. With his model of the student and teacher, it becomes evident that the inspiration occurs not only through words, but also through other forms of communication, such as through the language of one's bodily expressions and through the witness of one's personal actions.

The conclusions that Abraham draws from the teacher-student model of inspiration are as follows: inspiration is dynamic and requires the active participation of both agents involved; inspiration is oriented toward a better use of one's own faculties; there is no guarantee that the recipient of inspiration will not err concerning the content he or she receives; and the mindset of the recipient of inspiration will more than likely entertain similar notions as the one who initiated the inspiration.

The shortcoming of Abraham's position is the realization that whenever an analogy is employed, in addition to similarities there are also marked differences. Abraham uses the analogy of one human person (the teacher) inspiring another human person (the student), yet when carried over to the realm of biblical inspiration, we are faced with a divine person inspiring a human person. Additionally, whenever a human analogy is used in reference to God's act, the dissimilarities are more numerous than similarities. It is difficult to ascertain exactly what dimensions of Abraham's analogy may be properly predicated of God and to what extent the dissimilarities of the analogy may obscure its helpfulness.

Additionally, Abraham's student-teacher model provides an illustration of inspiration that is largely external. Whether we focus our attention on the verbal aspects of this inspiration, such as the teacher's words, or the nonverbal aspects of this inspiration, such as the teacher's enthusiasm, conviction, body language, rapport with the students, and so forth, the factors involved in inspiration are more social and cognitive than personal and experiential. Yet when we consider the act of God inspiring the authors of Scripture, there is much more involved than merely external elements; the charism of inspiration elevates the natural faculties of the authors well beyond their natural abilities, allowing them to receive and understand the revelation of God in a unique manner. Moreover, in the act of a teacher inspiring his or her students, experience tells us that the students also inspire the teacher. This is to say that the teacher does not remain the sole initiator of inspiration, nor do the students remain the sole recipients of inspiration, but a transitive relationship is formed. Although Abraham's model helps shed light onto the mystery of biblical inspiration, his model remains insufficient. As helpful as observations may be pertaining to the external aspects of inspiration, these aspects remain at the natural level. Only when we include the aspect of the inner light of the Holy Spirit supernaturally elevating the human faculties in the order of grace do we arrive at a more adequate model of biblical inspiration.

5
KERN R. TREMBATH AND AN EXISTENTIAL MODEL OF BIBLICAL INSPIRATION

Introduction

Kern Robert Trembath devoted his doctoral dissertation at the University of Notre Dame to the subject of biblical inspiration under the direction of Reverend James T. Burtchaell, CSC. His dissertation has since been published as *Evangelical Theories of Biblical Inspiration: A Review and Proposal* (New York: Oxford University Press, 1987). Prior to his current professorship at the University of San Francisco, Trembath taught theology at Notre Dame and at the Aquinas Center of Purdue University.

A member of the Anglican Communion and professed American Evangelical, Trembath offers a theology of biblical inspiration that maintains that any serious consideration of this doctrine must be anchored in a personal awareness and lived experience of the salvation merited for us by Jesus Christ. This orientation of Trembath's theology is indicative of his Evangelical heritage, which "discloses a greater implicit emphasis upon the experience of salvation in Jesus than upon cognitive, dogmatic and historical articulation of this experience."[1] The foundational theological principles assumed by Trembath are twofold: the Bible is the ultimate rule for the Christian life, and there is the necessity of a profession of faith that Jesus is indeed the savior of the world and ultimate sign of God's love for humanity.

The Nature of Biblical Inspiration

Often theologians employ the terms "biblical inspiration" and "divine inspiration" interchangeably, yet Trembath points out that these terms do not have the same meaning and therefore are not interchangeable. He posits three substantial hallmarks of biblical inspiration that distinguish it from the much larger category of divine inspiration.[2]

The first hallmark of biblical inspiration recognizes that biblical inspiration is a specific mode of divine inspiration. Although it is true that God touches all areas of our lives with his grace and that he continually offers to us his providential guidance, nevertheless we recognize that the Bible remains a specific (but not exclusive) locus of this inspiration. Frequently, it is when we are specifically meditating upon the sacred Scriptures that we consciously become aware of the presence of God in our lives. When we choose to act in a specifically Christian manner as a result of our encounter with the sacred page, this specific mode of divine inspiration, maintains Trembath, is properly said to be biblical inspiration. As can be seen, this position differs from the occasion of a person receiving the prompting of the Holy Spirit within the context of any of life's ordinary dimensions, such as watching a television program, resting, reading an influential (but noncanonical) work, and so forth. This latter situation truly involves the person being inspired at some level by God, yet since this inspiration is mediated through extrabiblical phenomena instead of through the Bible, Trembath identifies such inspiration as divine inspiration, not biblical inspiration. It becomes evident, then, that all biblical inspiration is a form of divine inspiration, yet divine inspiration does not limit its expression to the form of biblical inspiration.

The second hallmark proper to biblical inspiration is that biblical inspiration necessarily relates to salvation through Jesus Christ, since our redemption in Christ is at the summit of the biblical message. Trembath observes, "...the phrase 'biblical inspiration' is thus an abbreviated reference to 'the experience of salvation by God through Christ as mediated through the Bible.'"[3] Grounding his approach in what he refers to as the "transcendental subjectivism" of Karl Rahner, Trembath effectively displaces the primacy of scientific, literary, or historic considerations of biblical inspiration by substituting in their place the personal and communal experience of salvation. Although these external considerations can be collectively studied and measured as raw data, the experience of salvation transcends these cognitive dimensions and places the interior spiritual activity of the human person in the forefront of any other considerations.[4] Such a perspective properly reorients salvation away from mere intellectual propositions and Gnostic attitudes, and toward a moral attitude that must embrace and be appropriated by the entire human person.[5] Words may be the vehicles for inspiration, but according to Trembath, words cannot claim for themselves the attribute of inspiration; only persons can be inspired. He writes:

> The phrase "biblical inspiration" initially points not to the Bible but to Christian believers who have experienced salvation from God through the Bible....To discuss the inspiration of the Bible apart from the context of the saving activity of God is formally as moot as to discuss the inspiration of an artist who has never painted or a teacher who has never had students. All attempts to account for biblical inspiration which fail to rest upon the presence of salvation in the human recipient at best are only ambiguously Christian and at worst ground the specificity of Christianity in such nonreligious concepts as logic, interior feeling, historical accuracy, or the like.[6]

The acknowledgment that the Bible is the authority in discerning authentic experiences of salvation from illusionary ones is a third essential characteristic of biblical inspiration. Since the Bible, according to Trembath, is God's way of giving us a reliable and instructive written guide with a purpose of helping us to know how to attain salvation, it becomes the normative expression of divine inspiration. Religious experience that one receives is to be weighed against the experiences witnessed by the New Testament communities as evidenced in the Bible. Trembath maintains that such a system successfully verifies religious experience by an external source, thereby preventing a fatal identification of arbitrary or misleading interior experiences with a truly inspiring religious experience. The rationale behind this concept is the conviction that the Bible manifests the fundamental attitudes, beliefs, and worship structure of the Jewish and New Testament communities, and the way in which the early Christians experienced salvation would be essentially the same as for all people of every epoch. Supposing this line of reasoning to be correct, it seems to follow that any significant departure in a contemporary believer's experience of salvation from that of a believer living in the apostolic age would indicate a lack of an authentic experience of salvation in Jesus. The witness of the Bible, therefore, becomes the litmus test for the alleged presence of divine inspiration within the community of believers of any postapostolic age.

Deductivist and Inductivist Theories of Biblical Inspiration

A theologian driven by a deductivist approach to the theme of biblical inspiration accepts what is set forth in the biblical record as true without hesitation, even before one begins to study the Bible itself. The reverse of the deductive methodology is the inductive approach, which begins with the experience of the human person and progressively works its way to uncovering the resulting dogmatic facts concerning God, including the phenomenon of biblical inspiration. Inductive methodology places stress upon the human dimension of biblical inspiration (or any other supernatural operation of God) and excludes any theological theories that would undermine a true human element, such as a mechanical theory of inspiration.

Trembath clearly favors the inductivist approach, reflecting that theologians following a strictly deductive approach to the Bible tend to consider theories of biblical inspiration wholly independent of human perceptions and judgments, since their thinking is grounded in a priori data that are above criticism or reproach. From this methodological standpoint, the theologian attempts to unfold the biblical message as well as the merits of personal experience and other nonlogically verifiable characteristics of God's word. The revealed nature and activity of God that transcend the intellect's ability to judge become the context wherein questions may be raised and answered pertaining to biblical inspiration, which Trembath identifies as "arguably the most concrete instance of interaction between God and human beings."[7]

Since a properly biblical understanding of God postulates his absolute infallibility, the deductivist would not even consider the possibility of God or his word as found in the Bible to be untruthful. Those who utilize a deductive methodology recognize that they themselves are judged by the biblical record rather than being in a position to pass judgment upon it. In this context, believers are said to be thinking and experiencing rightly when their subjective judgments conform to what has been objectively revealed by God. Likewise, believers must reorient their subjective judgments and perceptions when such judgments contradict dogmatic truths about the nature of God and his revelation as communicated through the Bible.

Trembath views the general principles of a deductive approach to understanding biblical inspiration as unsatisfactory because too much stress is placed upon the biblical text and doctrines themselves, elevating the significance of the objective process of inspiration at the expense of the subjective experiences of those persons who are recipients of inspiration and the ecclesial communities to which they belong.[8] Furthermore, as we shall see, Trembath believes that doctrine must be informed by human religious experience, instead of a human religious experience taking on a role subordinate to doctrine. Perhaps Trembath subscribes to this position because a merely cognitive, factual study of the content of revelation may be likened to any other branch of scientific study, since even purely secular disciplines involve grasping and understanding factual content.

For Trembath, the believer's experience of salvation in Jesus must be the specific starting point for any study of biblical inspiration, which is also the distinguishing factor between sacred science (theology) and the natural sciences. The process of starting from what is least knowable by way of our human experience and leading up to what is most knowable through human experience—the methodology of the deductivists—is criticized by Trembath as moving in the wrong direction. For him, we ought to progress gradually from what is most knowable to us experientially to that which is least known experientially, in this case, the doctrine of God himself. In this way the essential hallmark of biblical inspiration centering upon the experience of salvation in Jesus Christ becomes the starting point of further discussion.

Inspiration and the Human Recipient

For Trembath and others, biblical inspiration involves the agent's life becoming transformed through the encounter with the biblical word as God's mercy, love, and call to eternal salvation are personally experienced. Both the individual dimension of inspiration (the agent) as well as the communal dimension (every agent is part of a greater ecclesial society) are highlighted. Trembath affirms, "…the concept of inspiration requires at least two mentally active agents and a medium. Apart from this structure, and apart from the initiating activity of one agent by means of the medium and the receiving activity of the other by means of that same medium, there can be no concept of inspiration."[9]

Since true human participation and activity are necessitated by Trembath's position, anthropological considerations are in order. Trembath points out, "…there simply is no single or unified anthropology to which all evangelicals in various denominations would subscribe,"[10] yet he also realizes that such lack of uniformity must not hinder his work. It is sufficient for him that he adopts an anthropological foundation to biblical inspiration in the Evangelical tradition to which most, although not all, Evangelicals can agree. To summarize this foundation: (a) any true anthropology must necessarily reference God; (b) of the visible world, human beings alone are created in the image and likeness of God, thereby indicating that "only human persons are able to think about thinking"[11] and "only human beings are able and responsible to make judgments concerning moral truth and falsity."[12]

Trembath identifies three stages through which a believing person receives biblical inspiration. First, the believer chooses to read the Scriptures in a spirit of openness to the ways in which it will have a positive change upon his or her life. Second, the believer attempts to integrate what he or she already knows with what is being newly discovered in the Scriptures pertaining to salvation. Third, the believer makes a judgment to accept and appropriate into his or her personal life that which was learned about both God and himself or herself through the encounter with the Scriptures. This process becomes the fruit of "biblical inspiration" between the second and third stages, namely, when the content of the Scriptures transcends the cognitively factual dimension by being actualized in a religiously transforming way. Religious facts are common to both canonical and noncanonical literature, yet the transformation brought about within the person in light of the connection between the objective facts in the biblical record and the person's present exigencies of life is crucial. Trembath sums up this threefold process as follows: "…the phenomena of biblical inspiration, as all other instances of inspiration, is one of recognition, enhancement, and response to a mediated message,"[13] which corresponds to each of the three steps outlined above.

As can be seen, this view of biblical inspiration goes beyond many of the ancient models of inspiration, which often maintain that the reader remain utterly passive and receptive to God's activity as mediated through the Bible. Trembath rediscovers the true active component to biblical inspiration, namely, the interpretation and actualization of the text. Only in consideration of this active dimension of biblical inspiration could Trembath comment that biblical inspiration "involves a person's learning more about himself or herself from reading the Bible and in the process coming to know more about God."[14]

The Means of Inspiration

The second aspect to the structure of revelation pertains to the words of the Bible, which serve as vehicles through which the believer is faced with a choice to enter more fully into the life of Christ. This perspective is indeed different from viewing the human agent as the vehicle to bring about an inspired written text.[15] Thus the Bible is understood to be a means, and not the endpoint, of biblical inspiration. "In other words, 'the inspiration of the Bible' refers to the enhancement which the Bible instrumentally causes in persons and not to the Bible itself as the terminus or locus of that enhancement."[16] As a part of this stage, Trembath briefly discusses the notions of the verbal inspiration of the Bible, plenary inspiration of the Bible, and the truthfulness of the Bible.

The Initiator of Inspiration

The third and final stage of biblical inspiration addresses God as the formal cause of inspiration. Trembath is largely indebted to Karl Rahner in adopting a framework that "seeks to account for how God is said to ground all acts of human knowing, and therefore inspire them, without thereby asserting either that persons cease to be persons or that God communicates directly and immediately with the human mind."[17] The first part of this statement affirms that human persons must be able to freely employ their human faculties (methods of speech, command of grammar, manners of expression, etc.) or else inspiration would have no substantial human component. Were the sacred authors mere secretaries, their supporting functions could easily be replaced. The second portion of the statement necessitates that God inspire the human agent via a medium rather than acting directly upon the mind of the sacred author.

The conclusion drawn is that all human acts of understanding are in themselves inspired by God, therefore it is not necessary to draw a distinction between the way in which the biblical authors were inspired compared with the way that believing Christians are inspired when they read the Scriptures. Trembath concludes, "In all knowing acts, it is appropriate to recognize and be thankful to God as the indirect and ultimate initiator of understanding. This is what is meant by divine inspiration."[18]

This framework, which Trembath refers to as "transcendental subjectivism," lies at the heart of his proposal for an authentic way of viewing the notion of biblical inspiration. Trembath observes, "If 'subjectivism' reflects Rahner's insistence that we begin our anthropological analysis with concrete human experience, 'transcendental' reflects his belief that such experiences will ultimately reveal how God and humans interact in all acts of knowing."[19] Such a philosophical approach escapes the criticisms waged against pure subjectivism because it consists of both internal and external referents, instead of being based upon an exclusive internal (privatist) ground.[20] The internal referent is, of course, the experience and understanding of the acting subject, while the external referent pertains to those objective factors that are able to assess the authenticity of the inner experience and knowledge. For the believer, God's revelation becomes the external referent, especially God's revelation as witnessed in the Bible.[21]

Concluding Reflections

In his study, Trembath has pointed out that the only way we as human beings can learn about God is to be taught by him, and it is through divine revelation that we are instructed by God. According to Trembath, since God inspires all acts of human understanding, the inspiration experienced by the authors of the Bible is essentially the same as the inspiration extended to the contemporary reader of the Bible in faith.

Further developing Abraham's teacher-student model of biblical inspiration, Trembath distinguishes three components of biblical inspiration: two mentally active agents and the Bible, which serves as the medium of inspiration. These three components correspond to the three components of Abraham's model: the activity of the student who listens to the teacher's instruction; the message of the teacher that is mediated to the student through the classroom presentation; and the identity of the teacher as the initiator and enabler of the process of inspiration. Building upon this example of inspiration in the natural order, Trembath develops a strongly personal theory of biblical inspiration.

The distinction of charisms operative in the process of biblical inspiration as noted in traditional Catholic theology is absent in Trembath's work, for example, the theological charisms that were involved with the inspiration of the biblical prophets; the biblical texts themselves; the inspiration of the Old Testament and New Testament communities; the various workings of God's inspiration throughout sacred history; and the working of the Spirit of God within the Church. The focus of Trembath's theory of biblical inspiration is almost exclusively upon the reader of Scripture.

Biblical inspiration, for Trembath, is not to be viewed as a unique charism given in the past to the authors of the Bible with the purpose of allowing them to communicate the truth of God (cf. *Dei Verbum*, 12) in a written form, but rather biblical inspiration refers to the present and ongoing activity of God, which gives to the believer the experience of new life and salvation in Jesus through prayerful use of the Scriptures.

The greatest weakness running through Trembath's theory is closely linked to his greatest strength: Trembath's work is centered upon the importance of the inspiration of the reader to the extent that he largely neglects many other aspects of biblical inspiration, including the inspiration of the text, the inspiration of the original authors, and the social extensions of biblical inspiration. Trembath's position elevates personal experience above that of objective doctrine and truth, resulting in a faith grounded in personal subjectivism rather than in the objective plans and truth of God. This exaggerated focus upon the reader of the Scriptures is a disadvantage to understanding the fuller picture of the charism of biblical inspiration in the life of the Church throughout history. Trembath's exclusive focus on the existential dimensions of biblical inspiration impoverishes historical, ecclesial, and textual aspects of biblical inspiration.

6

PAUL J. ACHTEMEIER ON BIBLICAL INSPIRATION AND AUTHORITY

Introduction

Paul J. Achtemeier is a Presbyterian biblical scholar and professor emeritus at the Union Theological Seminary and Presbyterian School of Christian Education in Richmond, Virginia. He formerly was the Herbert Worth and Annie H. Jackson Professor of Biblical Interpretation from 1979 until his retirement in 1997, and he served as past president of the Society of Biblical Literature. In 1985 he served as the first non-Catholic president of the Catholic Biblical Association.

Relating to the theme of biblical inspiration, Achtemeier proposes a theory that is grounded upon three components: tradition, the situation in which the audience finds itself, and the task of the respondent. Achtemeier's concept of biblical inspiration is one of a dynamic process with no artificial limitations placed upon the final author, the wording of the text itself, or the contemporary believer who meditates upon the Bible in faith. In this way he understands the "inspired" Bible to mean "that God spoke not only to our forebears in the history of Israel, and to the apostles in the founding generation of the Christian church, but that he also continues to address his people through its pages, as they are read in public worship and private devotions."[1] To restate Achtemeier's position, he understands biblical inspiration as a dynamic process with no limitations, which includes the dimensions of revelation, rereadings of the text in light of changing circumstances, inspiration, and the actualization of the biblical texts in the life of the ecclesial community.

Background

Achtemeier traces the concept of prophetic inspiration to the Old Testament period, and he points out that "the ancient Greeks were conscious of the fact that poets and philosophers possessed gifts denied to ordinary men and women, and they accounted for these gifts by claiming that such people were inspired by the nine Muses, who gave songs to poets and divine thoughts to philosophers."[2] Thus even in pagan antiquity, there existed the notion of human beings, with the help of a superior, divine power, able to accomplish things that would otherwise be too far above their natural human capacities. Achtemeier notes, however, that whereas the Greek conception of inspiration involved an alteration of consciousness on the part of the person being inspired, the Hebrew concept of prophecy did not necessarily include a concomitant loss of consciousness or personal reason. Whereas the Greek conception reduced the person receiving the inspiration to an almost puppetlike state, the Hebraic model preserved the possibility of inspiration being accompanied by a dialogue between the prophet and God.[3]

Achtemeier identifies examples of both of these perspectives within Hebrew thought vis-à-vis the Old Testament. He points to Jeremiah as a prophet who truly was conscious of his words and deeds as he was influenced by God, yet he can also point to portions of Ezekiel's ministry where it appears that he was "possessed" by God at the expense of the normal operation of his human faculties.[4] Achtemeier comments that this ecstatic form of prophecy seemed to be the most popular of the inspired-author models of inspiration used by the early Jewish and Christian writers and is the view held by most contemporary Christian scholars.[5]

Achtemeier acknowledges a weakness in both the inspired-author model and the inspired-text model in accounting for the various literary forms and personal literary styles of the authors. He notes that the model of instrumental causality, which is a combination of both the inspired-author and inspired-text theories, helps to explain the various literary genres employed in the Bible more so than the other two types of models. Since the Holy Spirit elevates rather than abrogates the power of the author's intellect, the words and styles can truly be those of the human author (as imperfect as they may be), while ensuring that everything expressed is properly the Word of God. This Aristotelian-based theory that was adopted during the Scholastic period was a major contribution to our understanding of biblical inspiration and continues to hold considerable influence in any discussion concerning biblical inspiration.

Two Contemporary Views of Inspiration

Addressing what he refers to as the liberal and conservative views of biblical inspiration, Achtemeier classifies the liberal view of inspiration as "a mixture of the word of God with the erring words of its human authors."[6] Those who maintain this view acknowledge that the Bible is a record of God's revelation, a record subject to the typical imperfections that characterize sinful humanity. According to this liberal view, errors in the Bible can be admitted, and often the Bible is seen as a masterpiece of human literature equal in stature to the works of Dante or Homer. The liberal view's definition of inspiration could be understood as follows: "The Bible as a whole was accomplished by an extraordinary stimulation and elevation of the powers of men who devoutly yielded themselves to God's will, and sought, often with success unparalleled elsewhere, to convey truth useful to the salvation of men and of nations."[7] Neither inspiration nor the authority of the Bible is called into question; they are simply limited in meaning to accommodate the human foibles and limitations of the Bible.

The interpretive principle at work within the liberal model of inspiration is rooted in one's experience. When portions of the Bible appear to contradict what we know through our modern experience of science, religions, history, and so forth, then that portion of the Bible is deemed inaccurate and unessential. Yet when the various statements of the Bible are verified by the reader's personal experience, then those statements are regarded as authoritative for the believer. The Bible's authority, therefore, is affirmed, but deemed to be inferior to that of critical human reason judging the veracity of what is read in the Bible compared with what is experienced in life.[8]

Assessing this liberal view, Achtemeier states, "...we are persuaded that such a view of Holy Scripture is not adequate for either public or private spiritual life."[9] He rejects the possibility of human experience being more authoritative than the Bible, as well as the implication that inspiration be understood as simply a heightened state of natural knowledge comparable to the natural insights of geniuses of various disciplines. Achtemeier rightly asks why we should find the Bible more authoritative than noncanonical religious or even secular literature that can appeal to the human heart and spirit more than some of the arguably dull passages found in the Bible, such as genealogies, dietary laws, and so forth.

Situated on the other end of the spectrum from the liberal view is the conservative view of the inspiration of the Bible. Whereas proponents of the liberal view begin their interpretation with the Bible itself as their starting point so that they can then postulate a theory of inspiration based on what is given in the Bible, the conservatives approach the Bible through the presupposition of God's truthfulness. The conservatives will not admit that the Bible has error, since God is supreme truth, and supreme truth cannot deceive.[10] "Such inerrancy means simply that the Bible is free from factual error in all its statements, down to the most minute and incidental details. Such freedom from error is not limited to religious affirmations or statements pertaining to divine matters or to morality. It covers all statements of any kind made anywhere in the Bible."[11] Thus without even looking at the Bible, conservatives already are convinced that it cannot err, and any alleged error that is found in the Bible is predicated of the human reader's inability to understand or to an inaccurate or faulty translation.[12]

Among the strengths of the conservative view is that it does not attempt to underestimate the divine character of the Bible, and among its weaknesses is the "defensive" approach that conservative exegetes often are constrained to take. Rather than simply admit error in the Bible and move on, the conservative scholars strive to explain how seemingly contradictory passages really are not so, and how a spiritual reading of the Scriptures may correct seemingly erroneous statements. Achtemeier notes, "…the debate about and defense of inerrancy, with its endless attempts to reconcile what are at best peripheral details, diverts attention from the central themes of Scripture."[13] Yet there is no consensus between these two views about the locus of inspiration, and it is to this question that we now turn.

The Locus of Inspiration

We have already seen in our study of Burtchaell the strengths and weaknesses of an author-centered view of biblical inspiration, a textual-based concept of biblical inspiration, the theory of content inspiration, and the theory claiming an inspiration of ideas. Achtemeier briefly addresses the shortcomings of each of these theories and proceeds to formulate his proposal, which involves the dynamic interrelationship among three essential components of biblical inspiration: tradition, situation, and respondent.

Achtemeier identifies tradition as the first essential component for a proper understanding of biblical inspiration. By tradition he denotes the "means of which the community understands itself in relation to its past"[14] and "the way generations within the community of faith, in Israel and in the church, sought to appropriate the experience of those who had gone before."[15] Such appropriation is made possible not solely through human recollection, but through the dynamic action of the Holy Spirit: "The continuing presence of that Spirit finds the vehicle for that presence precisely in the traditions that remind the community of the origin it had, and hence the goal it is to pursue. It is that use by the Spirit of God which makes those traditions inspired."[16] These inspired traditions function to both preserve the religious history of the past, as well as to present anew, according to the new exigencies of life, the message of salvation for the contemporary believer. This insight leads us to the second essential component of biblical inspiration, which is the situation in which the believer (who is always a part of a larger community) finds himself or herself.

When the situation of the believer changes, the traditions that orient the believer to God must also be reinterpreted to accommodate the new life-context of the believer, lest the Scriptures run the risk of being irrelevant to everyone except the original audience. For example, Achtemeier writes:

> When a nomadic Hebrew people moves in from the desert to take possession of Canaan, an agricultural land, the traditions of the desert must be reinterpreted in order to allow the community of nomads to remain faithful to its origins within the radically changed situation in which the nomads then find themselves. Evidences of that are clear in the collections of laws in the Pentateuch, and in the stories of the books of Joshua and Judges, as the nomadic tribes seek to find, within the structure of their old traditions, a new mode of organizing themselves while yet remaining the people of God summoned out of Egypt and to which he gave a promised land.[17]

Achtemeier also finds in Scripture examples of earlier traditions being reinterpreted to face the contemporary situation.[18] For
example, he cites the portrait of Christ as found in each of the
Gospels as being presented in a way to speak most powerfully to the
target audience, writing, "Far from having one fixed meaning which
remained the same for all time, the sayings of Jesus were evidently
regarded as capable of quite different meanings in different situations, and the author who collected those traditions used them to
make the theological point he or she thought necessary for those
who would read that Gospel."[19] He likewise draws attention to the
fact that the Old Testament quotations found in the New Testament
do not always agree with either the Septuagint or the Hebrew text,
but reflect a reinterpretation to face the needs of the hearers at hand,
such as Paul's use of Deuteronomy 30:12–13 in Romans 10:6.[20] In
all, cases, Achtemeier points to the continued vitality of the Old Testament traditions for Christians, observing:

> The sedimentation of a living tradition, which grew
> and changed with changing situations, our Bible is not
> an archive of dead, treasured memories of the past, but
> the record of living traditions which because of their
> origins continue to provide guidance, and the basis for
> ever-new interpretations for the community of faith
> right to the present day. It is the ever-changing response
> of tradition to new situation that has given to our
> sacred Scriptures the characteristics they display and
> which must be taken into account in any attempt to
> understand how they have been inspired.[21]

The final component for a proper understanding of biblical
inspiration is the respondent, who either crafts a new tradition
based on the collective experience of the community of believers,
or who identifies a preexistent tradition and reinterprets it to meet
the need of the community of believers. Achtemeier understands
the respondent in broad terms, referring to "anyone who con-

tributes to the formulation and reformulation of tradition in specific situations"[22] through the motivation (inspiration) of the Holy Spirit. Achtemeier illustrates that the first two components he proposes for a proper understanding of biblical inspiration, namely tradition and situation, are of little use without the respondent. Without a prophet, the new application of tradition to the current situation would simply not occur.[23] Without a historian, traditions would not experience reevaluation in the light of changing historical circumstances. Without an evangelist, the traditions about Jesus would never be organized into a coherent form to meet the needs of some community of faith.[24]

It appears clear that Achtemeier's understanding of the respondent may include the actual author of the particular book of the Bible (given a hypothetical situation of a particular book being authored solely by one individual), yet his perspective concerning the respondent also includes everyone who had a hand in the production of the book, irregardless of whether they were involved in the beginning, middle, end, or final redaction of the book. This view is significant, because it acknowledges the communal character of inspiration instead of being fixated upon one individual out of the community who produces a sacred text. Achtemeier here attempts to strike a balance between both the individual contributions of the biblical authors and the role of the community out of which the compilers, editors, redactors, authors, and everyone else who contributed to the production of the sacred text acted:

> To be sure, communities as such do not write books, individuals do. But to put the total weight of inspiration on that final individual who sets down the results of a long process of formulation and reformulation, as is the case when one understands inspiration on the prophetic model, is to make a mockery of the intimate relationship between Scripture and community and to deny to key individuals—Jesus, the prophets, apostles—their true

role in the production of inspired Scripture. It is not only the final assembler or compiler or author who shares in the inspiration which has produced Scripture. Rather, inspiration must be understood to be at work in all who have shaped, preserved, and assembled portions of the traditions contained in the several books.[25]

Inspiration and Authority

The issue of biblical authority is intimately connected with that of biblical inspiration, raising the question, "What is the nature of biblical authority?" Achtemeier considers several alternatives before proposing his perspective. First, he rules out the claim to authority stemming from biblical truthfulness, since "Scripture does not function authoritatively when it is understood as pointing to itself as the source of inerrant truth, because at that point it has given up its primary function as witness to a reality beyond itself."[26] Critical reasons for calling into question the truthfulness of the Bible put aside, Achtemeier maintains that biblical truthfulness cannot be a basis for authority because such a statement means that the authority of the Bible is internally, textually based and accessed through its literary form, rather than dependent upon a source outside of itself for its authority. Second, the authority of the Bible cannot be the result of the community out of which it grew, since such a view would impart solely a human authority to the Bible. Third, Achtemeier dismisses "the institution that collected the books and formed them into a canon"[27] as the basis for the Bible's authority. Assuming that he is here historically speaking of the Church, he correctly maintains that the Bible's authority consists in something other (or something more) than external ecclesial endorsement. Fourth, authority cannot be grounded in something wholly outside the Bible. Here Achtemeier points to those who claim that the Bible is authoritative once it has been demythologized and the "real Jesus" uncovered (e.g., the Jesus Seminar). Finally, Achtemeier maintains that one's religious experience in reading the Bible cannot be the basis for biblical authority: "The authority of Scripture functions not to validate human experience, however deceived, rather Scripture functions authoritatively when it corrects the experience of those who read its words, shaping that experience in terms of the reality to which it bears witness."[28]

The question still remains: What, then, is the basis of the authority of the Bible? Achtemeier responds, "To ask the canonical Scripture about authority is to be pointed to Christ, and thus to be pointed beyond Christ to the One who acted in him to redeem and judge the world."[29] Thus the authority of the Bible has its ultimate foundation in Jesus Christ, a derived authority that permeates the content of Scripture, encouraging the reader to always go beyond the written text to the living God who inspired it.[30]

Achtemeier stresses what we can term the "sacramental value" of the Bible, that it points to a reality outside of itself. For example, Achtemeier cites the example of Paul, who in his epistles clearly points to Christ as the source of his authority and not to himself; we see also in the authors of the Gospels an unwillingness to claim authority for themselves, manifested through the fact that the authors did not attach their names to them. Even Jesus Christ, in whom the authority of the Bible is grounded, points beyond himself to the Father as the source of his own authority.[31]

In more accessible terms for the modern reader, Achtemeier concludes his view of the authority of Scripture as follows: "On the most basic level, the authority of Scripture lies in its ability to *author* reality, that is, to create a certain identity previously nonexistent in those who hear its witness, and to bring into existence, and subsequently to renew, the fellowship of persons in whom such new identity has been 'authored,' namely, the Christian community."[32]

Concluding Reflections

Achtemeier set forth the main strengths and weaknesses of both the liberal and conservative models of biblical inspiration and built upon the positive aspects of each in developing his theory of biblical inspiration that hinges upon the threefold aspects of tradition, the situation, and the respondent. His focus on a living tradition corrects a view of biblical inspiration that sees in the Bible nothing more than a relic of past events. An acknowledgment of the situation (content) reminds us that the Word of God is not monolithic, but must be reinterpreted and applied to the specific, changing concrete life situations in which believers find themselves. Finally, considerations of the respondent take into account the diverse number of persons who have contributed to the transmission, interpretation, reinterpretation, and actualization of the biblical texts.

Of no less importance, Achtemeier addresses the problem of the origin of biblical authority and shows how the Bible's authority does not stem from its truthfulness, nor from an external imposition of authority by the communities from which it grew, nor by a decree of the Church rendering the Bible authoritative, nor through one's religious experience confirming what the Bible states. The authority of the Bible, teaches Achtemeier, has its ultimate foundation in Jesus Christ. Such a conclusion reveals that the Bible points toward a reality beyond itself for the purpose of directing us to Christ through its mediation.

Perhaps the most prominent weakness of Achtemeier's theory is that he encapsulates under the umbrella of one reality the multiple charisms that are included in a full understanding of biblical inspiration. To some, the charism of composition was given; to others, of interpretation; and yet to others, or reinterpretation according to the exigencies of the reader; and yet to others, the charism of discerning the Spirit's plan for their own personal lives, and so forth. Achtemeier groups these various charisms, which represent differing modes of inspiration, into one reality and labels it "biblical inspiration."

7
BIBLICAL INSPIRATION
AND THE EUCHARIST

A Proposal

Having surveyed what some of the most influential contemporary scholars have said about biblical inspiration, we wish to propose a unique insight into our theme, namely, that the Eucharist should be seen as a hermeneutic toward a fuller understanding of the doctrine of biblical inspiration.

It is at the eucharistic banquet that we encounter the source of our salvation most profoundly, and it is within the liturgy that the inseparable relationship between the Bible and the Eucharist is demonstrated.[1] The Fathers of the Second Vatican Council saw the need to expressly identify and communicate this essential relationship between the Eucharist and the Scriptures:

> The Church has always venerated the divine Scriptures just as she venerates the body of the Lord, since, especially in the sacred liturgy, she unceasingly receives and offers to the faithful the bread of life from the table both of God's word and of Christ's body. She has always maintained them, and continues to do so, together with sacred tradition, as the supreme rule of faith, since, as inspired by God and committed once and for

all to writing, they impart the word of God Himself without change, and make the voice of the Holy Spirit resound in the words of the prophets and Apostles.[2]

Pope Benedict XVI, writing as Joseph Ratzinger, illuminates the reason for the parallel between the Bible and the Eucharist, thereby pointing out the necessity of Scripture in the life of the Church:

> The liturgy of the word was not just a preliminary part of the Mass that could be more or less dispensed with, but of fundamentally equal value with the liturgy that is sacramental in the narrower sense; that the Church, as the community of the body of Christ, is definitely also the community of the Logos, living on the word, so that the "flesh" and "word" in which the "body of Christ," the word made flesh, comes to us becomes our "bread."[3]

Just as the Word of God accommodated itself to the authors of the two Testaments in human language, in the Eucharist we celebrate the Word of God coming among us, accommodating himself to our weakness by transforming ordinary bread and wine into himself.[4] That same glorified humanity is offered to us each time we partake of the Eucharist, enabling our experience of salvation to be enhanced through the same Spirit that inspired the early Church (including the biblical authors) and continues to inspire readers of the biblical word today.[5]

We looked at the doctrine of biblical inspiration in two dimensions: its unique, historical, objective importance and its subjective importance in the lives of Christians as they encounter Jesus Christ. Similarly, the Eucharist may be seen according to its objective and subjective dimensions, both of which are meaningful for the doctrine of biblical inspiration.

Of all the seven sacraments, only the sacrament of the Eucharist is made present upon the altar *ex opere operato* as a reality independent of the intention or disposition of the faithful who come to receive it, providing the priest employs the proper matter, form, and intention; the objective fact that the bread and wine have become the Body, Blood, Soul, and Divinity of Jesus is wholly independent of the spiritual disposition of the recipient of the sacrament.[6]

Similarly, the doctrine of biblical inspiration from the reference point of the biblical authors efficaciously accomplished its primary effect—the production of the written Scriptures—independent of the spiritual and existential states of the authors or the Christian communities to which or from which they wrote.

Yet the Eucharist, like the other six sacraments, also admits of a subjective dimension, namely, a personal increase in sanctity and communion with Christ *ex opere operantis*. In order for the fruits of this sacrament to be manifested to the individual communicant, he or she must approach the sacraments in the state of grace and in faith. Under this aspect, Jesus Christ enters into the souls of believers and meets them where they are, in the midst of the exigencies of life, with the continual offer of guidance and strength to attain eternal salvation. This is, in many ways, similar to the way in which the Holy Spirit inspires the believer through the Scriptures to be more faithfully committed to his service.

Granting the validity of these reflections, one might still inquire how the Eucharist can be viewed as a hermeneutic for understanding biblical inspiration. Let us consider P. J. Achtemeier's insight: "Scripture functions authoritatively when it functions as witness, pointing beyond itself to the reality of God as the final locus of truth."[7] In this sense we think also of St. Augustine, who remarked, "And thus a man who is resting upon faith, hope and love, and who keeps a firm hold upon these, does not need the Scriptures except for the purpose of instructing others."[8] The Bible's ultimate function is to point to a reality beyond itself. The propositional content of the Bible is not the terminus of biblical inspiration, but the medium that directs us to God, who has been made supremely accessible to us and died for us in the person of Jesus Christ.[9]

In Jesus Christ, we are given direct, not derivative, access to the Father. We are directed to Jesus Christ not abstractly, but through the concrete reality of his true Body and Blood, Soul and Divinity, which is made present upon the altar. It is in the reception of the Eucharist that we truly, substantially, concretely enter into communion with Jesus Christ, so that "through him, with him, and in him," we may enter into the eternal act of Christ's adoration toward the Father.

In the context of biblical inspiration, then, we suggest the following relationships: God originally inspired the sacred authors (including all contributors) to produce a truthful, written text for his people so that the drama of salvation history could be passed down in a fixed form to all generations. The purpose for such a text is sacramental, namely, to point beyond its pages to the Word of God, Jesus Christ, who is the source and goal of all inspiration through the Spirit, and who is accessible to us within the specific vehicle of the Church that he founded. This Church was empowered by the authority of God to act in his name, and therefore to make present via grace his saving power. Ultimately, the fount and summit of the Church is the Eucharist, which is the sacrament of the true, substantial presence of Jesus Christ on earth and ultimate mode of union with Christ in this life.[10]

Turning for a moment to an important pericope in the last chapter of Luke's Gospel, we are presented with the account of the two disciples who encountered Jesus on Easter Sunday evening while en route to Emmaus:

> Now on that same day two of them were going to a village called Emmaus, about seven miles from Jerusalem, and talking with each other about all these things that had happened. While they were talking and discussing, Jesus himself came near and went with them, but their eyes were kept from recognizing him. And he said to

them, "What are you discussing with each other while you walk along?" They stood still, looking sad. Then one of them, whose name was Cleopas, answered him, "Are you the only stranger in Jerusalem who does not know the things that have taken place there in these days?" He asked them, "What things?" They replied, "The things about Jesus of Nazareth, who was a prophet mighty in deed and word before God and all the people....Then he said to them, "Oh, how foolish you are, and how slow of heart to believe all that the prophets have declared! Was it not necessary that Christ should suffer these things and then enter into his glory?" Then beginning with Moses and all the prophets, he interpreted to them the things about himself in all the scriptures. As they came near the village to which they were going, he walked ahead as if he were going on. But they urged him strongly, saying, "Stay with us, because it is almost evening and the day is now nearly over." So he went in to stay with them. When he was at the table with them, he took bread, blessed and broke it, and gave it to them. Then their eyes were opened, and they recognized him; and he vanished from their sight. They said to each other, "Were not our hearts burning within us while he was talking to us on the road, while he was opening the scriptures to us?" (Luke 24:13–19; 25–32)

The illumination of the Holy Spirit that the disciples received in order to properly understand the prophecies and teaching of the Old Testament in light of Christ was occasioned through their contact with Jesus himself, who, on this occasion, explained how the Bible pointed to him and how he fulfilled the highest aspirations of Messianic hope. Yet the disciples did not recognize Jesus while he interpreted the Bible as being fulfilled in him, because their discussion was simply at an intellectual level. It was within the context of faith vis-à-vis the liturgy—the eucharistic celebration—that the disciples first recognized Jesus Christ. Once they recognized him through the "breaking of the bread," they reflected back that indeed their hearts "burned within them" as Jesus was interpreting the Scriptures for them. Commenting on this passage, Pope John Paul II wrote:

> It is significant that the two disciples on the road to Emmaus, duly prepared by our Lord's words, recognized him at table through the simple gesture of the "breaking of bread." When minds are enlightened and hearts are enkindled, signs begin to "speak." The Eucharist unfolds in a dynamic context of signs containing a rich and luminous message. Through these signs the mystery in some way opens up before the eyes of the believer. As I emphasized in my Encyclical *Ecclesia de Eucharistia*, it is important that no dimension of this sacrament should be neglected. We are constantly tempted to reduce the Eucharist to our own dimensions, while in reality *it is we who must open ourselves up to the dimensions of the Mystery.* "The Eucharist is too great a gift to tolerate ambiguity and depreciation."[11]

Biblical inspiration (objective), illumination and actualization (subjective), then, are not simply ordered to salvation in Jesus Christ in a general way, but concretely ordered toward the Eucharist as a privileged locus of the Holy Spirit's sanctifying activity.[12] John Paul II reminded us:

> There is therefore an objective relationship between Christ's paschal sacrifice and the gift of the Spirit. Since the Eucharist mystically renews Christ's redemptive sacrifice, one can easily see the intrinsic link between this sacrament and the gift of the Spirit. In founding

the Church through his coming on the day of Pentecost, the Holy Spirit established it in objective relationship to the Eucharist, and ordered it toward the
Eucharist.[13]

If the Church as a whole is directed and ordered toward the
Eucharist, as John Paul II states, then the Bible itself, which grew
out of the Church, cannot be ordered toward anything less. John
Paul II continues, "The Eucharist is the sacrament of this redemp-
tive love, closely connected with the Holy Spirit's presence and
action...,"[14] and the Spirit's presence and action manifests itself,
among other ways, in the illumination of the hearts of the believers as they contemplate the sacred page, and finds its culmination
in the worthy reception of the Eucharist.

The contemporary believer encounters and recognizes Jesus
in the Eucharist through the work of the Holy Spirit enkindling
the fire of faith. The "inspiration" of illumination that the believer
receives through meditating upon the Scriptures is ordained
toward and made supremely meaningful through the Eucharist, as
expressed by the Pontifical Biblical Commission: "In principle,
the liturgy, and especially the sacramental liturgy, the high point
of which is the Eucharistic celebration, brings about the most perfect actualization of the biblical texts, for the liturgy places the
proclamation in the midst of the community of believers, gathered around Christ so as to draw near to God."[15]

CONCLUSION

The Nature of Biblical Inspiration

Looking back upon the contributions offered by the scholars presented in this study, it would be helpful to recapitulate ten significant conclusions that have been reached to advance a more adequate understanding of biblical inspiration.

1. We recognize that the Bible is not merely a witness or record of revelation, but it is revelation itself; the Bible communicates to us the very words of God in the words of men, and is therefore properly called the Word of God. This fact acknowledges the validity of propositional revelation and bears witness to the fact that there is an inner unity within the words and the works of God as manifested in history. Historical events demonstrate what has happened, whereas statements by God mediated through the prophets and the other sacred authors of the Scriptures direct us toward the meaning and spiritual significance of those events in light of the universal call to salvation. It is fitting, then, that the Church acknowledges the Bible to be sacred, not just because of what it contains, but because of what it is. Instructive in this regard is *Dei Verbum* 2, where it is stated that the "plan of revelation is realized by deeds and words having an inner unity: the deeds wrought by

God in the history of salvation manifest and confirm the teaching and realities signified by the words, while the words proclaim the deeds and clarify the mystery contained in them."

2. In its most technical sense, the charism of biblical inspiration pertains to a free gift of the Holy Spirit given to selected, individual human persons in the past for the purpose of consigning the Word of God to a written form, that it could be known, preserved, and passed down to all generations. This gift of God is wholly unmerited by the recipients, it is ordered toward the good of the Church at large, and it directly acts upon the human faculties by elevating them and rendering them capable of receiving and understanding supernatural revelation. Yet one renders this objective dimension of inspiration deficient if, in accepting its validity, one at the same time rejects the subjective dimension of the Spirit's illuminative and ongoing transformative power within the life of the believer.

3. The same Spirit who inspired the sacred authors and who is the soul of the Church continues to work in the hearts of the faithful today. Although this type of inspiration by the Spirit is different in both kind and degree from the Spirit's mode of operation in the apostolic and preapostolic periods of the composition of the Scriptures, the Spirit nonetheless extends its graces to every human person, inspiring him or her to a greater commitment to the truth, which ultimately is grounded and perfectly revealed in Jesus Christ. In all cases, however, we must avoid the danger of reducing the objective content and structure of faith to personal subjectivism and religious experience. When taken together, these second and third points may prove helpful for ecumenism, since it is possible to affirm both the traditional Catholic and classical Protestant perspectives of biblical inspiration according to its objective and subjective dimensions.

4. The composition of the sacred Scriptures was a result of the mutual collaboration between God and man, each acting within his own proper role. God acts as the initiator of inspiration, and man, through his free cooperation, wrote those things and only those things that God wanted written for the sake of our salvation. Therefore the dual authorship of the sacred Scriptures is affirmed without in any way lessening the sovereignty of God or the freedom of man. Considering the many theories of biblical inspiration that have been suggested by the authors of this study, it seems that the theory of instrumental causality, analogously understood, still retains a pride of place as best expressing the phenomenon of biblical inspiration. This being said, it is important to point out that the Second Vatican Council also explicitly approves of the "incarnational model," as set forth in *Dei Verbum* 13:

> In Sacred Scripture, therefore, while the truth and holiness of God always remains intact, the marvelous "condescension" of eternal wisdom is clearly shown, "that we may learn the gentle kindness of God, which words cannot express, and how far He has gone in adapting His language with thoughtful concern for our weak human nature." For the words of God, expressed in human language, have been made like human discourse, just as the word of the eternal Father, when He took to Himself the flesh of human weakness, was in every way made like men.

5. It follows by logical necessity that the Bible is absolutely truthful, mindful of the proper application of biblical hermeneutics and understanding of literary genres, which, on the one hand, affirm that the Bible communicates the Word of God as accommodated to and expressed in human language that is subjected to critical study, yet on the other hand, maintain that the Bible must be interpreted according to the same supernatural and divine Spirit in which it was written. Since

God is the author of Scripture, any error would be predicated of him, and it is clearly impossible that God can err or purposely mislead his people into error.[1]

6. Many of our philosophical presuppositions for interpreting the Bible are built upon the Western Greek tradition, and such thinking has invaluably aided us in understanding the content of revelation. Although the philosophical mindset of the ancient Hebrews and the Near East was quite different from an Aristotelian perspective, the test of time has shown that the Aristotelian synthesis of metaphysics and epistemology, with the diversity of opinions that existed prior to Aquinas and were brought together by him, provides a firm grounding for continual dialogue between faith and reason, nature and grace.

7. The role of the magisterium is to authoritatively guard, interpret, and pass down to each generation the revelation of God as found in the twofold deposit of sacred Scripture and sacred tradition. Having received this most serious mission from Christ himself, the magisterium continues to serve the Church by advancing the work of theologians that properly witnesses to the truth and by correcting wayward opinions as a father corrects his children. Theologians, therefore, ought to submit their theological insights to the authority of the magisterium, realizing that there can never be a true contradiction between theological conclusions raised through an application of critical theories of exegesis and those conclusions that we hold to be true by faith. For this reason we also affirm that the most fruitful approach to the interpretation of the Scriptures consists in the confluent application of both the deductive and inductive methods.

8. The Bible in its entirety is equally inspired, both the Old Testament as well as the New Testament. This being said, it is also true that not all the passages in Scripture contain the same

theological, pastoral, or liturgical preeminence. While not suggesting that there is a "canon within the canon" by way of the degree of inspiration, one can, in fact, affirm that there are particular sections of the inspired texts that speak more loudly and more clearly to us both as individuals and as an ecclesial community than others. To state this point another way, we affirm that all portions of the Bible are equally inspired, yet the content can and does vary in degrees of importance, thereby corresponding to a varying potential of spiritual effectiveness when the reader interprets and actualizes the biblical text.

9. When we study terms found in the canonical corpus that were drawn from a context outside of Judeo-Christian revelation, we must be mindful of the fact that the meaning of the term may very well be different in Judeo-Christian usage than in traditions outside of this milieu. For example, the term for inspiration as found in the New Testament (*theopneustos*) was drawn from Hellenism, the meaning of which referenced the state of "divine madness" that a prophet was thrown into when receiving divine inspiration. Yet it is clear that the New Testament usage of this term does not accept the way in which it was previously used. It is suggested that the motive for using such a term was pragmatic; there was simply no terminology already in the Judeo-Christian tradition that could convey the concept that Paul was attempting to relate. Identifying the intention of the author and the way in which the author utilizes language is crucial for a proper understanding of the Scriptures.

10. The Bible's ultimate function, and therefore the function of biblical inspiration for the contemporary believer, is to direct us to Christ vis-à-vis the real, concrete encounter with him as we receive his Body, Blood, Soul, and Divinity in the Eucharist. The same Spirit who inspired the Bible is active and present in the world through the Eucharist, and only in the

light of the eucharistic Lord do the Scriptures take on their fullest significance for the believer in faith. In our reception of the Eucharist we discover the convergence of the historical with the timeless, of the objective Presence with our subjective dispositions, and our desire for union with Christ with its attainment. This insight opens new possibilities for ecumenical dialogue between Catholics and non-Catholic Christians in that it directly links the doctrine of biblical inspiration with the sacrament of the Body and Blood of Jesus, thereby pointing toward a more fruitful understanding of the richness of the doctrine of biblical inspiration and its implications for the Christian life.

NOTES

Introduction

1. Karl Rahner, *Inspiration in the Bible* (New York: Herder and Herder, 1961), 6.

2. James Barr, *The Scope and Authority of the Bible* (Philadelphia: Westminster Press, 1980), 1.

3. See James Barr, *The Bible in the Modern World* (New York: Harper and Row, 1973), 13.

4. Brevard Childs, *Biblical Theology in Crisis* (Philadelphia: Westminster Press, 1970), 87.

5. Paul J. Achtemeier, *Inspiration and Authority: Nature and Function of Christian Scripture* (Peabody, MA: Hendrickson Publishers, 1999), 2.

6. Barr, *The Bible in the Modern World*, 15.

7. In this study we employ the phrase *sola scriptura* according to its traditional meaning as stated by James Barr: "...that the Bible can and should be consulted on its own: apart on the one hand from any official church *magisterium*, and apart on the other hand from any overriding authority of the later interpretation of the biblical documents" (James Barr, *History and Ideology in the Old Testament* [Oxford: Oxford University Press, 2000], 53). Whereas the Protestant reformers crippled the role of tradition, Catholics maintain that the magisterium alone officially interprets the Word of God, thereby properly orienting the respective roles of both Scripture and tradition. "If, as noted above, the Scriptures belong to the entire Church and are part of 'the heritage of faith,' which all, pastors

and faithful, 'preserve, profess and put into practice in a communal effort,' it nevertheless remains true that 'responsibility for authentically interpreting the Word of God, as transmitted by Scripture and Tradition, has been entrusted solely to the living Magisterium of the Church, which exercises its authority in the name of Jesus Christ' (*Dei Verbum*, 10). Thus, in the last resort it is the Magisterium which has the responsibility of guaranteeing the authenticity of interpretation and, should the occasion arise, of pointing out instances where any particular interpretation is incompatible with the authentic Gospel" (*The Interpretation of the Bible in the Church* [Boston: Pauline Books and Media, 1993], 105).

Chapter One: Abraham Joshua Heschel on Prophetic Inspiration

1. In an interesting statement, Paul Achtemeier opines that the theory of principal and instrumental causality accepted by many conservatives as an adequate explanation for the relationship between the inspired biblical author and God maintained prominence for so long in history because of its connection with the prophetic model of inspiration (which is the subject of Heschel's study). Achtemeier writes, "the Aristotelian idea of a principal efficient cause found its best analogy and chief model in the biblical concept of 'prophet,' and it is in that form that this way of understanding inspiration has dominated theological reflections on the nature of inspiration to the virtual exclusion of all other forms" (Achtemeier, 15).

2. Abraham J. Heschel, *The Prophets*, vol. 2 (New York: Harper and Row, 1969), xi.

3. Abraham J. Heschel, *God in Search of Man* (New York: Farrar, Straus and Giroux, 1955), 258.

4. For example, Dewey Beegle writes, "Whereas, on the one hand, the concept of inspiration permeates the Bible, the biblical writers, on the other hand, do not give any psychological clues to explain how this inspiration took place" (*Scripture, Tradition and Infallibility* [Grand Rapids: William B. Eerdmans, 1973], 199).

5. Abraham J. Heschel, *The Prophets* (New York: Harper and Row, 1962), 24.

6. Ibid., 223.

7. Ibid., 25.

8. Ibid., 21.

9. Paul J. Achtemeier's exegesis of 2 Peter 1:20–21 in the context of Hebrew prophecy lends support to Heschel's position: "...the prophetic interpretation of various events Israel experienced in its history was due not to the prophet's own ideas but to ideas given to him by God. If Amos, for example, spoke of the doom of Israel, it was not because he somehow thought up that interpretation of present and future events by himself, but rather because he was moved to understand events in that way by God's own Spirit" (Achtemeier, 95).

10. Heschel, *The Prophets*, 24.

11. Abraham J. Heschel, *The Prophets*, vol. 1 (New York: Harper and Row, 1969), 6.

12. Heschel, *The Prophets*, vol. 2, 55.

13. Heschel, *God in Search of Man*, 136.

14. Heschel, *The Prophets*, vol. 2, 3.

15. Ibid., 57.

16. Ibid., 4.

17. Ibid., 100–101.

18. Ibid.

19. Ibid., 4.

20. Heschel, *The Prophets*, 257.

21. Ibid., 222.

22. Ibid., 247.

23. Ibid., 248.

24. Ibid., 260.

25. Ibid., 262.

26. Ibid., 271–72.

27. Ibid., 271 (emphasis added).

28. Ibid., 269.

29. Ibid., 268.

30. See Heschel, *The Prophets*, vol. 2, 48–49.

31. Heschel, *The Prophets*, 430.

32. Ibid., 431.

33. Heschel, *God in Search of Man*, 213.

34. Heschel, *The Prophets*, 431.

35. Ibid., 435.

36. Ibid., 440.

37. Ibid., 308.

38. See ibid., 443.

39. Asking a similar question, but from the perspective of the Bible's truthfulness rather than from its inspiration, Barr comments, "Inspiration ensured that the original autograph was without error. But what of what happened afterwards? And what of earlier drafts, previous editions, and of oral tradition from which reports were later taken to be written down?" (James Barr, *Fundamentalism* [Philadelphia: Westminster Press, 1977], 293–94).

40. Consider, for example, the thrust of John Paul II's encyclical, *Fides et ratio.*

41. Anselm, *Proslogion*, trans. S. N. Deane, in *Saint Anselm: Basic Writings* (La Salle, IL: Open Court, 1962), 2.

42. Homily 43: 7, 9 in Patrologia Latina 38: 257–58.

Chapter Two: J. T. Burtchaell on Catholic Theories of Biblical Inspiration

1. James Tunstead Burtchaell, *Catholic Theories of Biblical Inspiration Since 1810: A Review and Critique* (Cambridge: Cambridge University Press, 1969), 279.

2. Ibid., 281.

3. A similar position is shared by James Barr, who writes, "In this time [the nineteenth century] it would have been possible for Rome to accept fully the new types of knowledge, and to say that they would do no damage to the basic theological tradition of the Church. Rome, however, apparently out of sheer conservatism, then burdened itself with a series of rigidly backwards rulings which have been a source of difficulty to Roman Catholic scholars until very recent times" (Barr, *The Bible in the Modern World*, 16).

4. Until the early 1970s, the Pontifical Biblical Commission functioned as an organ of the magisterium. As such, the decisions of the PBC were binding. Subsequent to Paul VI's restructuring of the PBC in 1971, its nature was solely one of a consulting body within the Congregation for the Doctrine of the Faith.

5. Similarly hostile toward the authority of the Church, O. Weber considers the efforts of Scholasticism with respect to the development of the theory of biblical inspiration to have been minimal, because he believed any study under the guidance of the magisterial authority of the Church was necessarily deficient. See Bruce Vawter, *Biblical Inspiration* (Philadelphia: Westminster Press, 1972), 43.

6. Burtchaell, 88.

7. Ibid., 121.

8. Ibid., 105.

9. Achtemeier offers a specific objection to the theory of divine dictation grounded in the literary diversity found in the Bible and its imperfections: "If the Holy Spirit dictated every word, how can one account for differences in style and vocabulary? Above all, how can one account for infelicities of styles and grammar? Can God be the source of anything imperfect?" (Achtemeier, 21)

10. See Burtchaell, 93.

11. Ibid., 98.

12. Ibid., 13.

13. Ibid., 149.

14. Ibid., 127 (emphasis added).

15. See Leo XIII, *Aeterni Patris*, 1879.

16. Burtchaell, 123–24.

17. Ibid., 131–32.

18. St. Thomas Aquinas, *Summa Theologica*, trans. Fathers of the English Dominican Province (New York: Benziger Bros., 1948), II–II Q 174, art. 2, ad 3.

19. Burtchaell, 135.

20. Edmund Ford, "Inspiration," *The Tablet* 105 (1905): 44.

21. Burtchaell, 132.

22. Ibid., 133.

23. Lindsell observes, "…thoughts, when committed to writing, must be put into words. And if the words are congruent with the ideas, the words no less than the thoughts take on great importance. Words have specific meanings. To suppose that thoughts are inspired but the words that express them are not, is to do violence even to the thoughts" (Harold Lindsell, *The Battle for the Bible* [Grand Rapids: Zondervan, 1976], 33).

24. Paul Achtemeier summarizes the theory of instrumental causality and demonstrates some of its benefits as follows: "God, the principal efficient cause, so motivated and inspired the biblical author, the instrumental efficient cause, that the author's potential for writing intelligible language was used for purposes, and to write materials, which the author alone could not have done. In that way, one could account for the writings that had obviously been written by human beings, yet that would say more than human beings by themselves could have conceived or composed. The analogy had the additional advantage that it would enable one to account for Scripture coming ultimately from God, yet written in thoroughly human thought categories. God moves as principal efficient cause in such a way that the human potential and faculties of the author are in no way subverted or destroyed. Such 'inspiration,' so it was argued, does not cancel human potentiality so much as it raises it. In that way human potentiality becomes capable of more than it could realize if left to its own devices" (Achtemeier, 12).

25. Burtchaell, 163.

26. Ibid., 296.

27. Ibid., 303. James Barr offers quite a different outlook: "...one of the great traditional terms applied to scripture is misleading. It is wrong to think of scripture as a 'record': it is not in essence a record, though in places it may incidentally be so. Even in its past narratives its function is often not to be a record of past events but to present paradigms for thinking about the present or hoping for the future" (Barr, *The Scope and Authority of the Bible*, 36).

28. Barr, *The Scope and Authority of the Bible*, 36.

29. Burtchaell, 291.

30. John Paul II, in his reception of the PBC document, "The Interpretation of the Bible in the Church," directly called to mind the incarnational analogy found in *Divino afflante Spiritu*, no. 37: "For as the substantial Word of God became like to men in all things, 'except sin,' so the words of God, expressed in human language, are made like to human speech in every respect, except error." Not all scholars, however, accept this Christological-incarnational analogy of the two natures of Christ being applied to the divine and human aspects of the Bible. For example, James Barr asserts, "There is, for instance, no good reason why the relationship between God and man in the person of Christ should be supposed to hold good also for the relationship of divine and human in the

Bible; even if one accepts in the fullest way a formula like the Chalcedonian about the person of Christ, there is no reason why it should be applicable also to the Bible (for which, needless to say, it was not designed)" (Barr, *The Bible in the Modern World*, 22).

31. Bloesch offers a similar assessment, "In biblical religion error means swerving from the truth, wandering from the right path, rather than defective information (See Prov 12:28; Job 4:18; Ezek 45:20; Rom 1:27; 2 Pet 2:18; Jas 5:20; 1 Jn 4:6; 2 Tim 2:16–19)," in *Holy Scripture, Revelation, Inspiration and Interpretation* (Downers Grove, IL: InterVarsity Press, 1994), 107.

32. As is quite evident today, the magisterium welcomes the honest application of the critical methods of biblical interpretation, provided that the practitioners of these methods do not employ philosophical or theological presuppositions that are false.

33. The following extended excerpt is taken from *The Interpretation of the Bible in the Church*, 102–3: "Thus all the members of the Church have a role in the interpretation of Scripture. In the exercise of their pastoral ministry, *bishops*, as successors of the apostles, are the first witnesses and guarantors of the living tradition within which Scripture is interpreted in every age. 'Enlightened by the Spirit of truth, they have the task of guarding faithfully the Word of God, of explaining it and through their preaching making it more widely known' (*Dei Verbum*, 9; see *Lumen Gentium*, 25). As co-workers with the bishops, *priests* have as their primary duty the proclamation of the Word (*Presbyterorum Ordinis*, 4). They are gifted with a particular charism for the interpretation of Scripture, when, transmitting not their own ideas but the Word of God, they apply the eternal truth of the Gospel to the concrete circumstances of daily life (ibid.). It belongs to *priests* and to *deacons*, especially when they administer the sacraments, to make clear the unity constituted by word and sacrament in the ministry of the Church....The Spirit is, assuredly, also given to *individual Christians*, so that their hearts can 'burn within them' (*Luke* 24:32) as they pray and prayerfully study the Scripture within the context of their own personal lives. This is why the Second Vatican Council insisted that access to Scripture be facilitated in every possible way (*Dei Verbum*, 22; 25). This kind of reading, it should be noted, is never completely private, for the believer always reads and interprets Scripture within the faith of the Church and then brings back

to the community the fruit of that reading for the enrichment of the common faith."

Chapter Three: Bruce Vawter on Social Inspiration

1. Summarizing the relationship between social inspiration and the traditional view of inspiration, Barr writes, "Traditional theology had always taught that the Bible was, in a sense, a community production: it was the voice of ancient Israel, the voice of the apostolic church. But, perhaps even more, it was the voice of great individuals, of Abraham, Moses, Isaiah, Jeremiah, Daniel, Jesus, and St. Paul. Their utterances could, perhaps, be integrated by interpretation with traditional theology. This individual emphasis was deeply affected by biblical criticism, even more again as form criticism developed, and most of all, finally, as more and more attention devoted to the social aspects of biblical religion" (Barr, *History and Ideology in the Old Testament*, 111).

2. Bruce Vawter, *Biblical Inspiration* (Philadelphia: Westminster Press, 1972), 8.

3. Ibid., 3.

4. Ibid., 2.

5. Ibid., 4–5.

6. Ibid., 5.

7. Ibid., 8.

8. Ibid., 9.

9. Ibid., 9–10.

10. Ibid., 10.

11. Ibid., 48.

12. Ibid., 128.

13. Ibid., 13.

14. Ibid., 15.

15. Ibid., 18. On the emphasis upon the reality instead of upon the words that communicate it, Dewey Beegle writes, "Moreover, 'verbal' exactness is not to be expected in quotations [from the Old Testament], because the interest of the New Testament writers centered in the *sense, not the exact wording* of the Old Testament source. In effect, then, the term 'verbal' is

broadened so as to refer ultimately to the ideas rather than to every word" (*Scripture, Tradition and Infallibility*, 235).

16. Vawter, 18.

17. Ibid., 162.

18. See ibid., 162–63.

19. Ibid.

20. See ibid.

21. Ibid., 45.

22. Dewey Beegle apparently overlooked the significance of the theory of instrumental causality as proposed by Aquinas in stating, "For over a thousand years after Jerome and Augustine there was little change in the formulation of the doctrine of inspiration" (*Scripture, Tradition and Infallibility*, 138).

23. Vawter, 48.

24. This is not to say that the theory of instrumental efficient causality is the only possible theory of biblical inspiration that a Catholic theologian could hold in good conscience, nor do we imply that there may never be proposed in the future a theory more accurate to the phenomena of biblical inspiration than that of instrumental causality.

25. Vawter, 57.

26. Ibid., n. A, 77.

27. Ibid., 79.

28. See ibid., 85.

29. Ibid., 58.

30. Ibid., 107.

31. Ibid., 168.

32. Ibid., 157.

33. Ibid., 168.

34. Ibid., 158.

35. James Barr notes, "The Bible is in its origin a *product* of the believing community. Modern biblical study has made this much more plain to us than it could ever have been in the past. Traditional doctrines of scripture suggested to Christians over many centuries that the Bible was a message *from* God *to* the community. And of course we can still say this, but we can say it only more indirectly: in the sense, perhaps, that scripture grew out of the tradition of the believing community, but, having so grown, became in its turn the Word of God to the community" (*The Scope and Authority of the Bible*, 113).

36. Vawter, 159.
37. Ibid., 162.

Chapter Four: W. J. Abraham and Divine Inspiration According to Human Analogy

1. His publications include: *Canon and Criterion in Christian Theology* (Oxford: Clarendon Press, 1998); *Waking from Doctrinal Amnesia* (Nashville: Abingdon Press, 1995); *The Logic of Evangelism* (Grand Rapids: Eerdmans, 1989); *The Rationality of Religious Belief*, edited with Steven W. Holtzer (Oxford: Clarendon Press, 1987); *Divine Revelation and the Limits of Historical Criticism* (Oxford: Oxford University Press, 2000); *An Introduction to the Philosophy of Religion* (Englewood Cliffs, NJ: Prentice-Hall, 1985); *The Divine Inspiration of Holy Scripture* (New York: Oxford University Press, 1981).

2. Abraham, *The Divine Inspiration of the Holy Scripture*, 91.

3. Ibid., 7.

4. Ibid., 58.

5. Ibid., 60.

6. Ibid., 61.

7. Ibid., 84.

8. Ibid., 86.

9. Ibid., 90.

10. Ibid., 59–60.

11. See ibid., 63–64. The insights that follow are primarily Abraham's, with extended explanations offered by myself.

12. See ibid., 64–65.

13. Ibid., 65.

14. Ibid., 68, 69–70.

15. See ibid., 72.

16. For example, Abraham writes that his proposal, in contradistinction to a deductivist proposal, leaves an open question as to "whether Jonah was an historical figure or not" and "how far the Gospel of John is chronologically accurate." For him it is a grave mistake to approach the text believing that it is without error. We might mention, however, that such a conviction, namely, that it is wrong to approach the text believing

that there are no errors in it, is itself the manifestation of a deductive principle.

17. Abraham, 118.

Chapter Five: Kern R. Trembath and an Existential Model of Biblical Inspiration

1. Kern Robert Trembath, *Evangelical Theories of Biblical Inspiration* (New York: Oxford University Press, 1987), 4.

2. Trembath actually provides four criteria to distinguish biblical inspiration from divine inspiration; however, the third and fourth criteria appear to be virtually identical in expression and they overlap in content. To simplify matters, I have combined these two criteria, which he identifies as hallmarks three and four, into one criterion addressed as hallmark number three.

3. See Trembath, *Evangelical Theories*, 111.

4. While it is true that any religious text written by a layperson has the potential to challenge and inspire a person to conversion, Trembath makes the point that the only way to truly learn *about God* is to learn *from God*, since his ways are far beyond human understanding. Only the Scriptures are able to teach us about God through the words of God himself as expressed by the sacred authors, and therefore of all written records of salvation, the canonical texts stand in a uniquely privileged position.

5. According to Trembath, although many theologians claim that the propositions stated in the Bible are inspired (in an objective genitive sense), they in themselves are not inspiring (in the subjective genitive sense), and therefore Trembath concludes that these propositions are an insufficient basis for biblical inspiration.

6. Trembath, *Evangelical Theories*, 114–15.

7. Kern Robert Trembath, *Divine Revelation: Our Moral Relation with God* (New York: Oxford University Press, 1991), 11.

8. For Trembath, the authoritative Bible still remains a human product, not a divine one.

9. Ibid., 90.

10. Ibid., 75.

11. Ibid., 77.

12. Ibid., 78.

13. Trembath, *Evangelical Theories*, 81.

14. Ibid., 85.

15. According to Trembath's model, the words of the Bible are not in themselves inspired, since only personal subjects are capable of receiving and acting through inspiration. Trembath remarks, "In challenging the adequacy and coherence of theories of inspiration which assume that inspiration is located in the words of the Bible rather than in the lives of believers, we are challenging the meaning of the concept of inspiration as that meaning has been understood in most of Jewish and Christian tradition" (*Evangelical Theories*, 70).

16. Ibid., 103.

17. Ibid., 106.

18. Ibid., 109.

19. Ibid., 106.

20. See ibid., 105.

21. Yet a difficulty arises if we go another step and ask if the Bible is supposed to objectively assess human experience, then what is supposed to ensure that the individual's understanding of the Bible is itself free from subjectivism, in the absence of any authoritative body that interprets the Bible for us?

Chapter Six: Paul J. Achtemeier on Biblical Inspiration and Authority

1. Paul J. Achtemeier, *Inspiration and Authority: Nature and Function of Christian Scripture* (Peabody, MA: Hendrickson Publishers, 1999), 8.

2. Ibid., 16.

3. For an excellent study on the understanding of divine inspiration within ancient Greek drama and poetry through the lenses of Plato, Plutarch, and Julian, see Allen R. Hunt, *The Inspired Body* (Macon, GA: Mercer University Press, 1996), chapter 1.

4. Achtemeier, 17–18. In these pages Achtemeier also gives some other examples of situations where prophets seemed totally possessed by God: 1 Sam 10:5–6, 10–13; 19:23–24; 1 Kgs 18:12, 46; 2 Kgs 2:16.

5. See ibid., 19.

6. Ibid., 31.

7. Ibid., 32.

8. The insights taken here are partly those of L. H. DeWolf, cited and explained by Achtemeier in pages 32–33.

9. Ibid., 36.

10. Explaining the term "error" as employed by the conservatives, Achtemeier writes, "Error, as the word is used in this sense, does not refer to such trivial matters as a misspelled word or a mistake in grammar. Rather, an error is understood to be a misstatement or something contrary to fact" (ibid., 39).

11. Achtemeier, 38.

12. We think of Augustine here.

13. Achtemeier, 62.

14. Ibid., 108.

15. Ibid., 131.

16. Ibid., 111.

17. Ibid., 112.

18. Achtemeier's evaluation of the importance of biblical tradition and its reinterpretation for the present is also shared by the Pontifical Biblical Commission's *The Interpretation of the Bible in the Church*, which states "The texts of the Bible are the expression of religious traditions which existed before them. The mode of their connection with these traditions is different in each case, with the creativity of the authors shown in various degrees. In the course of time, multiple traditions have flowed together little by little to form one great common tradition. The Bible is a privileged expression of this process: it has itself contributed to the process and continues to have controlling influence upon it....One thing that gives the Bible an inner unity, unique of its kind, is the fact that later biblical writings often depend upon earlier ones. These more recent writings allude to older ones, create 're-readings' (*relectures*) which develop new aspects of meaning, sometimes quite different from the original sense" (*The Interpretation of the Bible in the Church*, 89–90).

19. Achtemeier, 70. Compare with the teaching of *Dei Verbum*, no. 19: "For, after the ascension of the Lord, the apostles handed on to

their hearers what he had said and done, but with that fuller understanding which they, instructed by the glorious events of Christ and enlightened by the Spirit of truth, now enjoyed. The sacred authors, in writing the four Gospels, selected certain of the many elements which had been handed on, either orally or already in written form, others they synthesized or explained with an eye to the situation of the churches, sustaining the form of preaching, but always in such a fashion that they have told us the honest truth about Jesus."

20. Explaining this example, Achtemeier writes, "Instead of using this passage [Dt. 30:12–13] to show, as Deuteronomy did, that superhuman efforts are not necessary in order to fulfill the commandments of the law, since it is not some reality remote from the covenant community, Paul uses the passage to justify his claim that it is precisely that performance of the law which the coming of Christ has rendered useless in God's eyes. In using the tradition from the Old Testament with such freedom, Paul is doing nothing different from the way we have seen other biblical authors and compilers using older traditions" (Achtemeier, 73).

21. Achtemeier, 115.

22. Ibid., 116.

23. Consider the observation by Sanders, "…some of the oldest material in the Bible, as received, contemporized tradition for a new (ancient) situation. From our point of view, the prophets, who are frequently thought of as original thinkers and even as spontaneous oracles in their own right, are now seen to be citing, either directly or by allusion, authoritative traditions of the communities to which they spoke" (James A. Sanders, *Canon and Community: A Guide to Canonical Criticism* [Eugene, OR: Wipf and Stock, 1984], 27).

24. Achtemeier, 116.

25. Ibid., 117–18. Compare with Barr: "Scripture emerged from the tradition of the people of God. Now there is no reason why we should say that the scripture, i.e., the final written product, is inspired by God but the stages which led up to it, in which the important decisions were taken, the stages of oral tradition and the like, were not inspired by God. So inspiration would have to be understood in the sense that God and his Spirit was in and with his people in the formation, transmission, writing down and completion of their tradition and its completion and fixation as scripture" (Barr, *The Scope and Authority of the Bible*, 63).

26. Achtemeier, 146.

27. Ibid.

28. Ibid., 146–47.

29. Ibid., 144.

30. Compare with the position of James Barr: "Authority resides in the people of God, or perhaps more correctly in the central leadership of the people of God; but it also resides in the scripture which they formed and passed on to later generations as their own communication, as the voice which they wanted to be heard as their voice" (*The Scope and Authority of the Bible*, 64).

31. Achtemeier, 144–45.

32. Ibid., 151.

Chapter Seven: Biblical Inspiration and the Eucharist

1. "Catholic Christianity is centered on the Eucharist, and it is in the perspective of the Eucharist that the Bible should be considered. All use of Scripture in the Church should be regarded as being explicitly or implicitly related to the Mass. All readings or hearing of God's word is an act of sacred memory, bringing to life God's marvelous deeds in the past that have culminated in Christ" (James Swetnam, "The Word of God and Pastoral Theology in the Contemporary Church," in *Vatican II: Assessment and Perspectives: Twenty-Five Years After (1962–1987)*, ed. René Latourelle (Mahwah, NJ: Paulist Press, 1988), 365).

2. *Dei Verbum*, no. 21.

3. Joseph Cardinal Ratzinger, "Sacred Scripture in the Life of the Church," in Herbert Vorgrimler, *Commentary on the Documents of Vatican II*, vol. 3 (New York: Crossroad Publishing Company, 1989), 263. See also John Paul II, *Mane nobiscum Domine*, October 7, 2004, no. 12.

4. "In this sacrament of bread and wine, of food and drink, everything that is human really undergoes a singular transformation and elevation. Eucharistic worship is not so much worship of the inaccessible transcendence as worship of the divine condescension, and it is also the merciful and redeeming transformation of the world in the human heart" (John Paul II, *Dominicae cenae*, February 24, 1980).

5. "The primitive Church was a community founded on the teaching of the apostles (Acts 2:42). It was completely animated by the Holy Spirit who enlightened the believers to understand the Word, and gathered them together in charity around the Eucharist. Thus the Church grew into a multitude of believers who 'were of one heart and soul' (Acts 4:32)" (John Paul II, "The Intrinsic Link Between the Eucharist and the Gift of the Holy Spirit," General Audience, September 13, 1989).

6. Recall, for example, that for all of the remaining six sacraments, their validity is not only contingent upon the proper matter, form, and intention of the minister, but also on the inner attitude of the recipient. If a person receiving any of these six sacraments were to will against their respective ends, then the sacrament would be rendered invalid.

7. Achtemeier, 146.

8. St. Augustine, *On Christian Doctrine*, Nicene and Post-Nicene Fathers, series I, vol. II (Grand Rapids: Eerdmans, reprinted 1993), 534.

9. Although it is true that the Bible makes God accessible to us, it does so in a derivative way insofar as it is not through its pages alone that we encounter God, but only when the reader approaches the Bible in an attitude of faith offered to us through the Holy Spirit.

10. "The Eucharist is the summit of the whole Christian life because the faithful bring to it all their prayers and good works, their joys and sufferings. These modest offerings are united to the perfect sacrifice of Christ. Thus they are completely sanctified and lifted up to God in an act of perfect worship which brings the faithful into the divine intimacy (See Jn 6:56–57). Therefore, as St. Thomas Aquinas writes, the Eucharist is 'the culmination of the spiritual life and the goal of all the sacraments' (*Summa Theol.*, III, q. 66, a. 6)" (John Paul II, "The Eucharist Is the Source of the Church's Life," General Audience, April 8, 1992).

11. John Paul II, *Mane nobiscum Domine*, 14.

12. "At the center of the Church is the Eucharist, where Christ is present and active in humanity and in the whole world by means of the Holy Spirit" (John Paul II, "The Intrinsic Link Between the Eucharist and the Gift of the Holy Spirit," General Audience, September 13, 1989).

13. Ibid.

14. Ibid.

15. *Interpretation of the Bible in the Church*, 124.

Conclusion

1. Unfortunately, there are more than a few scholars who misinterpret *Dei Verbum*'s teaching on biblical inerrancy. A discussion of this issue goes beyond the scope of this study; however, careful consideration of footnote 5 of *Dei Verbum* no. 11 makes clear that indeed Vatican II reaffirmed the plenary inerrancy of the Bible and did not endorse the theory of partial inerrancy that some of the Council Fathers had suggested.

SELECTED BIBLIOGRAPHY

Abbott, Walter M., ed. *The Documents of Vatican II*. New York: Guild Press, 1966.

Abraham, William J. *The Divine Inspiration of Holy Scripture*. New York: Oxford University Press, 1981.

———. "Inspiration, Revelation and Divine Action: A Study in Modern Methodist Theology." *Wesleyan Theological Journal* 19 (1984): 38–51.

Achtemeier, Paul J. *Inspiration and Authority: Nature and Function of Christian Scripture*. Peabody, MA: Hendrickson Publishers, 1999.

Ahern, Barnabas. "Scriptural Aspects." In *Vatican II: An Interfaith Appraisal*, 54–67. Notre Dame, IN: University of Notre Dame Press, 1966.

Alonso Shökel, Luis. *The Inspired Word: Scripture in the Light of Language and Literature*. Translated by Francis Martin. New York: Herder and Herder, 1965.

Anselm. *Proslogium*. Translated by S. N. Deane in *Saint Anselm: Basic Writings*. La Salle, IL: Open Court, 1962.

Aquinas, Thomas. *Summa Theologica*. Translated by the Fathers of the English Dominican Province. 5 vols. New York: Benziger Brothers, 1948.

Artola, Antonio M., and José M. S. Caro. *Bibbia e parola de Dio*. Brescia: Paideia Editrice, 1994.

Balentine, Samuel E., and John Barton, eds. *Language, Theology, and the Bible: Essays in Honour of James Barr*. Oxford: Clarendon Press, 1994.

Barr, James. *The Bible in the Modern World*. New York: Harper and Row, 1973.

————. *Fundamentalism*. Philadelphia: Westminster Press, 1977.

————. *History and Ideology in the Old Testament*. Oxford: Oxford University Press, 2000.

————. *Holy Scripture: Canon, Authority, Criticism*. Philadelphia: Westminster Press, 1983.

————. *The Scope and Authority of the Bible*. Philadelphia: Westminster Press, 1980.

Barton, John. *Holy Writings, Sacred Text: The Canon in Early Christianity*. Louisville: Westminster John Knox Press, 1997.

Bea, Augustin. *The Word of God and Mankind*. Chicago: Franciscan Herald Press, 1967.

Beegle, Dewey M. *Scripture, Tradition and Infallibility*. Grand Rapids: William B. Eerdmans, 1973.

Begbie, Jeremy. "Who Is This God—Biblical Inspiration Revisited." *Tyndale Bulletin* 43:2 (1992): 259–82.

Benedict XV. *Spiritus Paraclitus*. September 15, 1920.

Benedict XVI. Homily on the occasion of the closing of the Twenty-Fourth Italian National Eucharistic Congress. May 29, 2005.

————. Homily on the occasion of taking possession of the Cathedral of Rome. May 7, 2005. Text cited from "Presiding in Doctrine and Presiding in Love." *L'Osservatore Romano* (English Edition), May 11, 2005: 3–4.

Benoit, Pierre. *Aspects of Biblical Inspiration*. Translated by J. Murphy-O'Connor and S. K. Ashe. Chicago: Priory Press, 1965.

Berkouwer, Gerrit C. *Holy Scripture*. Grand Rapids: William B. Eerdmans, 1975.

Bloesch, Donald G. *Holy Scripture: Revelation, Inspiration and Interpretation*. Downers Grove, IL: InterVarsity Press, 1994.

Boice, James M. *Standing on the Rock: Biblical Authority in a Secular Age*. Grand Rapids: Baker Books, 1994.

Brown, Raymond E., and Thomas Aquinas Collins. "Church Pronouncements." In the *New Jerome Biblical Commentary*, 1166–74. 1990.

Brown, Raymond E. *The Critical Meaning of the Bible*. Mahwah, NJ: Paulist Press, 1981.

Burtchaell, James T. *Catholic Theories of Biblical Inspiration Since 1810: A Review and Critique*. Cambridge: Cambridge University Press, 1969.

Bush, L. Russ, and Tom J. Nettles. *Baptists and the Bible: The Baptist Doctrines of Biblical Inspiration and Religious Authority in Historical Perspective*. Chicago: Moody Press, 1980.

Butler, Christopher. "The Constitution on Divine Revelation." In *Vatican II: An Interfaith Appraisal*, 43–53. Notre Dame, IN: University of Notre Dame Press, 1966.

Cameron, Nigel M. de S. "Inspiration and Criticism: The Nineteenth Century Crisis." *Tyndale Bulletin* 35 (1984):129–59.

Canale, Fernando L. *Back to Revelation-Inspiration: Searching for the Cognitive Foundation of Christian Theology in a Postmodern World*. New York: University Press of America, 2001.

Catechism of the Catholic Church, Second Edition. Washington, DC: United States Catholic Conference—Libreria Editrice Vaticana, 1997.

Childs, Brevard. *Biblical Theology in Crisis*. Philadelphia: Westminster Press, 1970.

Denzinger, Henry. *The Sources of Catholic Dogma*. Translated by Roy J. Deferrari. St. Louis: B. Herder, 1957.

Donahue, John. Review of *Catholic Theories of Biblical Inspiration Since 1810*, by James Burtchaell. *Church History* 39 (1970): 260–61.

Draper, James T., Jr. *Authority: The Critical Issue for Southern Baptists*. Old Tappan: Fleming H. Revell, 1984.

Dulles, Avery R. *Models of Revelation*. Maryknoll, NY: Orbis Books, 1992.

Flannery, Austin, ed. *Vatican Council II: The Conciliar and Post-Conciliar Documents*, vol. 1. New York: Costello Publishing, 1975.

Gamble, Harry. *The New Testament Canon*. Philadelphia: Fortress Press, 1985.

Gnuse, Robert. *The Authority of the Bible: Theories of Inspiration, Revelation and the Canon of Scripture*. New York/Mahwah, NJ: Paulist Press, 1985.

Goldenjay, John. *Models for Interpretation of Scripture*. Grand Rapids: William B. Eerdmans, 1995.

Grech, Prospero. "Quid est veritas? Rivelazione e ispirazione: nuove prospettive." La 'Dei verbum' Trent 'anni dopo: Ed. Nicola Ciola. 1995, 147–58 (Lateranum no. 2–3).

Grillmeier, Alois. "The Divine Inspiration and the Interpretation of Sacred Scripture." In H. Vorgrimler, ed., *Commentary on the Documents of Vatican II*, vol. III, 199–246. New York: Herder and Herder, 1969.

Harrington, Wilfrid J. *Record of Revelation: The Bible.* Chicago: Priory Press, 1965.

Harrisville, Roy A., and Walter Sundberg. *The Bible in Modern Culture: Theology and Historical Critical Method from Spinoza to Käsemann.* Grand Rapids: William B. Eerdmans, 1995.

Helseth, Paul K. "'Re-Imagining' The Princeton Mind: Postconservative Evangelicalism, Old Princeton, and the Rise of Neo-Fundamentalism." *Journal of the Evangelical Theological Society* 45:3 (2002): 427–50.

Hellín, Francisco G. *Concilii Vaticani II Synopsis: Constitutio Dogmatica De Divina Revelatione, Dei Verbum.* Vatican City: Libreria Editrice Vaticana, 1993.

Henry, Carl. *Revelation and the Bible: Contemporary Evangelical Thought.* Grand Rapids: Baker Books, 1958.

Heschel, Abraham J. *Between God and Man: An Interpretation of Judaism.* New York: The Free Press, 1959.

————. *God in Search of Man: A Philosophy of Judaism.* New York: Farrar, Straus and Giroux, 1955.

————. *The Insecurity of Freedom: Essays on Human Existence.* New York: Farrar, Straus and Giroux, 1966.

————. *The Prophets.* New York: Harper and Row, 1962.

————. *The Prophets*, vol. 1. New York: Harper and Row, 1969.

————. *The Prophets*, vol. 2. New York: Harper and Row, 1969.

Hodge, Charles. *Revelation and Inspiration.* New York: Oxford University Press, 1927.

————. *Systematic Theology*, vol. 1. New York: Scribner, 1871.

Hodges, Louis I. "Evangelical Definitions of Inspiration: Critiques and a Suggested Definition." *Journal of the Evangelical Theological Society* 37:1 (1994): 99–114.

Hoffman, Thomas A. "Inspiration, Normativeness, Canonicity, and the Unique Sacred Character of the Bible." *Catholic Biblical Quarterly* 44 (1982): 447–69.

Holmes, Derek J., ed. *The Theological Papers of John Henry Newman on Biblical Inspiration and Infallibility*. Oxford: Clarendon Press, 1979.

Hunt, Allen R. *The Inspired Body: Paul, the Corinthians, and Divine Inspiration*. Macon, GA: Mercer University Press, 1996.

L'interpretazione della Bibbia nella Chiesa. Atti del Simposio promosso dalla Congregazione per la Dottrina della Fede. Vatican City: Libreria Editrice Vaticana, 1999.

The Interpretation of the Bible in the Church. Boston: St. Paul Books and Media, 1993.

John Paul II. *Dominicae cenae*. February 24, 1980.

———. *Ecclesia de Eucharistia*. April 17, 2003.

———. "The Eucharist Is the Source of the Church's Life." General Audience, April 8, 1992.

———. *Fides et ratio*. September 14, 1998.

———. "The Intrinsic Link Between the Eucharist and the Gift of the Holy Spirit." General Audience, September 13, 1989.

———. *Mane Nobiscum Domine*. October 7, 2004.

Kelsey, David H. *Proving Doctrine: The Uses of Scripture in Modern Theology*. Harrisburg, PA: Trinity Press International, 1999.

Latourelle, René, ed. *Vatican II: Assessment and Perspective: Twenty-Five Years After (1962–1987)*. New York/Mahwah, NJ: Paulist Press, 1988.

Lee, Anthony D., ed. *Vatican II: The Theological Dimension*. USA: The Thomist Press, 1963.

Leo XIII. *Aeterni Patris*. August 4, 1879.

———. *Providentissimus Deus*. November 18, 1893.

Lindsell, Harold. *The Battle for the Bible*. Grand Rapids: Zondervan, 1976.

MacArthur, John F., Jr. "Evangelicals and Catholics Together." *The Master's Seminary Journal* 6:1 (1995): 7–37.

Mannucci, Valerio. *Bibbia come Parola di Dio*. Brescia: Queriniana, 2000.

Marshall, I. Howard. *Biblical Inspiration*. Vancouver: Regent College Publishing, 2004.

Martin, Marty E. "Tübingen Models for Theology." *Church History* 100 (1983): 653–56.

McKenzie, John J. "The Social Character of Inspiration." *Catholic Biblical Quarterly* 2 (1962): 115–24.

Miller, John H., ed. *Vatican II: An Interfaith Appraisal.* International Theological Conference. Notre Dame, IN: University of Notre Dame Press, 1966.

Minear, Paul S. "A Protestant Point of View." In *Vatican II: An Interfaith Appraisal,* edited by John H. Miller, 68–88. Notre Dame, IN: University of Notre Dame Press, 1966.

Montague, George T. *Understanding the Bible.* New York/Mahwah, NJ: Paulist Press, 1997.

Montgomery, John W. *The Suicide of Christian Theology.* Minneapolis: Bethany, 1971.

Muller, Richard A. "Giving Direction to Theology: The Scholastic Dimension." *Journal of the Evangelical Theological Society* 28:2 (1985): 183–93.

Nettleton, David. *Our Infallible Bible.* Schaumburg, IL: Regular Baptist Press, 1977.

Newman, John H. *On Biblical Inspiration and Infallibility.* Oxford: Oxford University Press, 1979.

Nineham, Dennis E. *The Use and Abuse of the Bible.* London: Macmillan, 1976.

Nix, William E. "The Doctrine of Inspiration Since the Reformation, Part II: Changing Climates of Opinion." *Journal of the Evangelical Theological Society* 27:4 (1984): 439–57.

O' Collins, Gerald. "Revelation Past and Present." In *Vatican II: Assessment and Perspective: Twenty-Five Years After (1962–1987),* ed. René Latourelle, vol. 1, 125–37. New York/Mahwah, NJ: Paulist Press, 1988.

Pache, René. *The Inspiration & Authority of Scripture.* Translated by Helen I. Needham. Salem: Sheffield, 1969.

Pannenberg, Wolfhart. "Theological Table Talk: On the Inspiration of Scripture." *Theology Today* 54:2 (1997): 212–15.

Pinnock, Clark H. *The Scripture Principle.* Vancouver: Regent College Publishing, 1984.

Pius XII. *Divino afflante Spiritu.* September 30, 1943.

Preiss, Théo. "The Inner Witness of the Holy Spirit." *Interpretation* 7 (1953): 259–80.

Rahner, Karl. *Inspiration in the Bible.* New York: Herder and Herder, 1961.

Ratzinger, Joseph. "Revelation Itself." In H. Vorgrimler, ed., *Commentary on the Documents of Vatican II.* Vol. 3, 170–80. New York: Herder and Herder, 1969.

Rogers, Jack, ed. *Biblical Authority.* Waco: Word Books, 1977.

Ruokanen, Miikka. *Doctrina Divinitus Inspirata: Martin Luther's Position in the Ecumenical Problem of Biblical Inspiration.* Helsinki: Luther-Agricola Society, 1985.

Rynne, Xavier. *Vatican Council II.* New York: Maryknoll, 1968.

Sanders, James A. *Canon and Community: A Guide to Canonical Criticism.* Eugene, OR: Wipf and Stock, 1984.

———. *From Sacred Story to Sacred Text: Canon as Paradigm.* Eugene, OR: Wipf and Stock, 1987.

Schaff, Philip, ed. *The Nicene and Post-Nicene Fathers.* Edinburgh: T. & T. Clark, Series I and II, 29 vols.

Seitz, Christopher R. "Biblical Authority in the Late Twentieth Century: The Baltimore Declaration, Scripture-Reason-Tradition, and the Canonical Approach." *Anglican Theology Review* 75:4 (1993): 470–86.

Sundberg, Albert C., Jr. "The Bible Canon and the Christian Doctrine of Inspiration." *Interpretation* 29 (1975): 352–71.

Swetnam, James. "The Word of God and Pastoral Theology in the Contemporary Church." In *Vatican II: Assessment and Perspectives: Twenty-Five Years After (1962–1987),* edited by René Latourelle, 364–81. New York/Mahwah, NJ: Paulist Press, 1988.

Tábet, Michelangelo. *Teologia della Bibbia: Studi su ispirazione ed ermeneutica biblica.* Roma: Armando, 1998.

Tracy, Robert. *American Bishop at the Vatican Council: Recollections and Projections.* New York: McGraw-Hill, 1966.

Trembath, Kern R. *Divine Revelation: Our Moral Relation with God.* New York: Oxford University Press, 1991.

———. *Evangelical Theories of Biblical Inspiration: A Review and Proposal.* New York: Oxford University Press, 1987.

Vanhoye, Albert. "The Biblical Question of Charisms." In *Vatican II: Assessment and Perspectives: Twenty-Five Years After (1962–1987),* edited by René Latourelle, 439–68. New York/Mahwah, NJ: Paulist Press, 1988.

Van Kooten, Tenis. *The Bible: God's Word.* Grand Rapids: Baker Books, 1972.

Vawter, Bruce. *Biblical Inspiration.* Philadelphia: Westminster Press, 1972.

Vorgrimler, Herbert, ed. *Commentary on the Documents of Vatican II,* vol. 3. New York: Herder and Herder, 1989.

Waller, Charles H. *The Authoritative Inspiration of Holy Scripture.* Greensboro: Rainbow Publications, 1973.

Warfield, Benjamin B. *The Inspiration and Authority of the Bible.* London: Marshall Morgan & Scott, 1951.

Wenger, John C. *God's Written Word: Essays on the Nature of Biblical Revelation, Inspiration and Authority.* Scottdale, PA: Herald Press, 1966.

Williams, Joel S. "Inerrancy, Inspiration and Dictation." *Restoration Quarterly* 37 (1995): 158–77.

Williamson, Peter S. *Catholic Principles for Interpreting Scripture: A Study of the Pontifical Biblical Commission's* The Interpretation of the Bible in the Church. Rome: Pontificio Instituto Biblico, 2001.

Wright, J. Robert. "The Official Position of the Episcopal Church on the Authority of Scripture, Part I: Present Teaching and Historical Development." *Anglican Theological Review* 74:3 (1992) 348–61.

Wright, J. Robert. "The Official Position of the Episcopal Church on the Authority of Scripture, Part II: Ecumenical Comparison." *Anglican Theological Review* 74:4 (1992): 478–89.

Young, Edward J. *Thy Word Is Truth: Some Thoughts on the Biblical Doctrine of Inspiration.* Grand Rapids: William B. Eerdmans, 1957.

Other Books in the Series

Other Books in the Series

What Are They Saying About Theological Method?
    by J. J. Mueller, SJ
What Are They Saying About Mark?
    by Daniel J. Harrington, SJ
What Are They Saying About the Letter to the Hebrews?
    by Daniel J. Harrington, SJ
What Are They Saying About John? (Revised Edition)
    by Gerard S. Sloyan
What Are They Saying About the Historical Jesus?
    by David B. Gowler
What Are They Saying About Fundamentalisms?
    by Peter A. Huff
What Are They Saying About the Universal Salvific Will of God?
    by Josephine Lombardi
What Are They Saying About Paul and the End Time?
    by Joseph Plevnik, SJ
What Are They Saying About the Letter of James?
    by Alicia J. Batten